GW00992194

CONTENTS

INTRODUCTION

In his infinite creativity, God is employing a vast array of methods and situations to build my family's trust upon himself. Not least of these is the responsibility he has placed upon me to teach from his word. As I have read the scriptures for any given topic, I have become acutely aware that I am preparing to teach about matters that God is using my experiences first to teach me. This inseparable link between what he has given me to pass on, and its relevance to my own daily living has been most reassuring.

The following is a collection of such topics, compiled over ten years. These include:

> Fruitfulness
>
> Spiritual warfare
>
> Judgement
>
> Personal choice and responsibility
>
> God's sovereignty
>
> Servant-heartedness
>
> True Joy

I trust that the work God has done in me through these passages of scripture, he will use to benefit those who read this book.

I have found God to be most consistent and diligent in cultivating a grand harvest from small seeds. My prayer is that the seeds sown through this book will grow to produce much fruit for the kingdom of God.

THE FRUIT OF THE SPIRIT
Genesis 1:28 & Galatians 5:22 - 25

But the fruit of the Spirit is love, joy, peace, forbearance, kindness, gentleness and self-control. Against such things there is no law. Those who belong to Christ Jesus have crucified the flesh with its passions and desires. Since we live by the Spirit, let us keep in step with the Spirit.[1]

*****

D o you know the very first words that God says to Adam and Eve in the Bible...?

"Be fruitful..."[2]

The Bible records that, over anything else, the first thing God wanted to communicate to mankind was this ... BE FRUITFUL! Here is a subject of tremendous importance in the Christian life.

And its not about having lots of babies. God said, "be fruitful AND multiply." Fruitfulness is the bearing of fruit - the growth and display of productive qualities in our day to day life. I hope to impress upon you now the *criticality* of this topic.

Fruitfulness is a theme that links all the major events in the Bible. God created the vegetation to bear fruit, the fish and birds to be fruitful. He told mankind to be fruitful. Fruit was their diet. Noah, Abraham, Jacob, Joseph, the Israelites in Egypt – all called and made to be fruitful. The first book of the Bible says, 'Hey, understand that fruitfulness is a crucial topic.'

The promised land is described by its fruit, - flowing with milk and honey. The spies prove it's desirability, by bringing back a sample.

They gave Moses this account: "We went into the land to which you sent us, and it does flow with milk and honey! Here is its fruit."[3]

The laws of Leviticus,[4] and Deuteronomy[5] speak of blessings and curses for Israel's conduct, in terms of fruit. 'If you follow my decrees and are careful to obey my commands,' God says... 'The fruit of your womb, and of your land and of your livestock will be blessed.' But for disobedience, 'The fruit will be cursed' (paraphrased).

Now, we know that where there is an instruction from God, there is perversion from the devil. Satan tempted Adam and Eve with *forbidden* fruit. Cain killed Abel because of his jealousy, aroused by the fruits they offered to God. Abraham was enticed away from the promised land and his promised offspring by the fruitfulness of the country and servant girl of Egypt.

Throughout scripture we see this recurring theme: Heaven's fruit that we are called to pursue in obedience to God's instruction, and worldly fruit offered us by the devil's deception. The two are opposed, and there is no middle ground. We must choose.

The matter of physical fruit in the Old Testament foreshadows a greater revelation and fulfilment in the New Testament – Spiritual fruit. If fruitfulness was significant then, so much more now!

The topic echoes throughout Psalms, proverbs, song of songs, and the prophets, and climaxes with Isaiah foretelling that,

"A shoot will come up from the stump of Jesse; from his roots a Branch will bear fruit.[6]

Israel will bud and blossom and fill all the world with fruit,[7]

and once more God's people will take root on Earth and bear fruit in Heaven."[8]

This shoot is Jesus, and his chosen people are prophesied to bear spiritual fruit for the kingdom.

Let's look at Jesus, and His miraculous healing of a blind man:

> ...some people brought a blind man and begged Jesus to touch him. He took the blind man by the hand and led him outside the village. When he had spit on the man's eyes and put his hands on him, Jesus asked, "Do you see anything?" He looked up and said, "I see people; I see them as trees walking around." Once more Jesus put his hands on the man's eyes. Then his eyes were opened, his sight was restored, and he saw everything clearly.[9]

First the man sees people like trees walking around. Then Jesus fully restores the man's sight. Jesus did not need two attempts to heal this man. He did not say to the dead man Lazarus, "Come out," only for Lazarus to call back from the tomb... "Well, my top half is back from the dead, but there's no feeling from the waist down. If you could now fix my legs, I'll be right out!"

Jesus had the power to restore the man's sight immediately. This two part healing was deliberate, and meant to reveal a heavenly truth. There is something in what the man first saw, that speaks of the spiritual state of the people around him. He saw people in the form of a tree - a form that could clearly reveal their fruit.

Here is the process: The blind man's friends brought him to Jesus so that Jesus could touch him. This Greek word for touch, means 'attach to.' Jesus then led the man out of the village, separating him from his normal worldly surroundings. He then enabled the man to see.

> "I see people; I see them as trees walking around."

Here we have two different Greek words meaning to 'see.' First the man declares "I see people." This verb for seeing is 'to see physically, but with spiritual understanding.' He then says, "I see them as trees" - A second Greek word for 'seeing,' which means to see with the mind, not the eyes; to see them 'spiritually.' The man could still not see physically, but he saw people spiritually as trees. Only then did Jesus open the man's eyes, so he saw everything clearly.

This is what we need to let Jesus to do for us. To allow him to attach himself to us, lead us out of the life we knew, help us see ourselves and others as fruit bearers, and then to see everything clearly. We need to see everything with 20-20 spiritual vision.

We are all bearing fruit. To regularly imagine ourselves walking around as trees and consider the fruit we bear, would be of great advantage to us. If I saw myself as a tree, I could better see the quality and the amount of the fruit I'm bearing. I might better know how my life looks to God and to others. I could see what God has done in me. I could see what branches in my life needed pruning. If I could see others as trees, I might better discern whether I should desire similar fruit as theirs, or stay well clear in case their rotten fruit infects my own.

John the Baptist addresses Pharisees and Sadducees, the leaders of religion, as a brood of vipers. He asks them,

> *"who warned you to flee from the coming wrath? Produce fruit in keeping with repentance."[10]*

John says, for all your religiosity there is no good fruit, only proof of your allegiance to Satan. A harsh rebuke! And one that should challenge us to inspect our own fruit very carefully. To fashion our salvation with fear and trembling.[11]

6

You see,

- Being devout isn't sufficient.
- Being a leader isn't sufficient.
- Family line or nationality isn't sufficient.
- Knowing scripture isn't sufficient.
- Observing festivals or attending church isn't sufficient.
- Even prophesying, driving out demons and performing miracles in Jesus' name is not sufficient. It proves the power of the name of Jesus, but not a person's standing before Him.

You can have all this and still be a bad tree, bearing bad fruit! Jesus himself called these 'religious leaders' snakes; a brood of vipers.[12] He warns us:

"Watch out for false prophets. They come to you in sheep's clothing, but inwardly they are ferocious wolves. By their fruit you will recognize them.... Every good tree bears good fruit, but a bad tree bears bad fruit... Every tree that does not bear good fruit is cut down and thrown into the fire."[13]

He says also,

"I tell you that the kingdom of God will be taken away from such people, and given to a people who will produce kingdom fruit."[14]

Every good tree bears good fruit. There are two Greek words used here for 'Good.' The 'goodness' of the tree is an inherent goodness, originating from God. An inner goodness, whether seen or unseen. So, you might see a stranger walking down the road and not know from their appearance whether that person is saved; or 'good'. But the goodness of the fruit is a different Greek word. It is an outward sign of the goodness within. It is obvious – seen to be good, attractive, desirable. It inspires others to embrace what is lovely!

People are looking for something to root their lives in. We who are saved are ambassadors of Christ.[15] People might not tell that from how we look, but we should live in such a way that anyone who spends any time with us should see how we live and want to embrace that life for themselves.

The matter of bearing fruit for the kingdom of God is inseparable from Christian living. We must look like Christ to attract people to him; bearing his fruit and making evident the reality and desirability of our faith. By this, we'll give people something far more substantial than mere words to convince them to root.

And we are called to make disciples of those who do root in Christ, *showing* them how to live by our example; by our fruit. Paul says,

> "*Therefore I urge you to imitate me.... my way of life in Christ Jesus, which agrees with what I teach everywhere in every church.*"[16]

Are we those who have allowed God to prune us such that we can say to others "Live like me, as I imitate Christ!" This is achievable for us when the Holy Spirit in us helps us to understand the importance of his fruit, and to pursue it with diligence!

There are two Greek words for the bad tree, with it's bad fruit. The badness of the tree is its rottenness, worthlessness, Corruption. And its bad fruit... full of labours, annoyances, and hardships. This world grows trees that walk around slumped under the weight of cares, troubles, broken relationships, grievances. Fruit of the world! If you recognise these fruits in your life, seek God with urgency to get his pruning sheers on you.

More than that. A good tree cannot bear bad fruit.[17] If you bear the fruit of the world, you prove there is something deeper that needs dealing with. No good asking God to take away bad fruit, but remain a bad tree!

Christians are not to carry worldly fruit. It is shaken off through true repentance. We hang all worldly fruits on Calvary's tree, we leave these grave clothes in the tombs of our crucified selves, so that we can get on living like Christ. If we speak of Christ but bear none of his fruit, people aren't going to want him. I could give the most eloquent speeches about God, but if my life does not bear heaven's fruit, pleasing to the eye of the non-believer, they won't want it.

On one tree, there is peace, love, Joy, faithfulness. And on the other? Annoyances, labours and hardships. If we as Christians keep hold of those weights, where is the evidence of our salvation? Our freedom? Where is the attraction to the Christian life? To Christ?

Don't get me wrong. Jesus said,

> "In this world you will have troubles, but take heart, I have overcome the world." [18]

People will hate you for following Christ. Trials, persecution - expect them all. But be overcomers, like Christ.

- God will keep in perfect peace those whose minds are steadfast, because they trust in him.[19]
- Do not conform to the pattern of this world, but be transformed by the renewing of your mind.[20]
- Consider it pure JOY when you face trials of many kinds for the fruit that it achieves.[21]
- We're considered as sheep to be slaughtered, and yet, in all these things we are more than conquerors.[22]

- When we are cursed, we bless; when we are persecuted, we endure it; when we are slandered, we answer
kindly.[23]
- As servants of God, we commend ourselves in every
way: in great endurance; troubles, hardships and dis-
tresses; in beatings, imprisonments and riots; in hard
work, sleepless nights and hunger [but] in purity, understanding, patience and kindness, in the Holy Spirit and
in sincere love, in truthful speech and in the power of
God; with weapons of righteousness in the right hand
and the left.[24]

This is Kingdom fruit.

We aren't called to be deliriously happy in all circumstances...
but to not react to trials with the fruits of persistent annoyance
and doubt. "By their fruit you shall know them." We either bear
the fruit of the Spirit, testifying to our new life in Christ, or we
bear the fruit of the world and are fit only for the fire.

- Is our fruit that of the Spirit, or the world?
- Do our branches bear the fruit of faithfulness, or mistrust?
- Do they bend under the weight of our love for others, or
strain under our irritation of them?
- Is our tree decorated with compassion and gentleness,
or burdened with annoyance and harshness?
- Do we wear peace and joy like fine jewellery, or stress
and misery like an anvil around our necks?
- Are patience and self control ripe upon our branches, or
rashness and greed rotting in our lives?

We are meant to be trees that bear splendid fruit as we live these
lives, to show that we are rooted in something worthwhile. And
our splendour is for his glory.

Jesus said,

> "I am the vine and you are the branches. If you remain in
> me, and I in you, you will bear much fruit, apart from me,
> you can do nothing." [25]

The fruit is a product of the life that originates in the vine and flows into the branch. It flows through Jesus into the Christian, so that our fruit is his, and his fruit is ours! A gift and evidence of a life grafted into his. The fruit of repentance, the fruit of the Spirit.

God has made these available to us. Yet that ancient serpent still lurks today, spinning his deception. "Did God really say to have joy? Come and eat from the tree of anxiety. Did He really say you can have self-control – wouldn't you prefer the fruit of over indulgence? Did God really say not to worry, not to gossip, not to love yourself first? Did God really say have unity? forgive? Why not keep chewing on anger, pride, jealousy, disunity?"

Listen,

> "If you are offering your gift at the altar and there remem-
> ber that your brother or sister has something against you,
> leave your gift there in front of the altar. First go and be rec-
> onciled to them; then come and offer your gift." [26]

This is a command, and it is serious. Whenever you come to God, you are coming to the altar. If you come with prayers, songs, financial offerings – either corporately or privately - and yet you know that to a brother or sister you have failed to show love, patience, kindness, goodness, gentleness or self-control, I'm serious, leave you money in your wallets, don't pray or sing another word. Go and put your relationships right.

It is better to have a church empty on Sunday morning because the whole congregation are out seeking reconciliation with their brothers, than to have a church packed to the rafters with a people who tolerate disunity and unforgiveness. By their actions they make themselves hypocrites - a prime reason people hate church.

If someone is seeking God and comes into a church only to see us treat each-other like people do out there in the world... They don't want that, they've had enough of it. God's own people will have put them off of seeking him. That's why Jesus was so angry with the Religious leaders. That is why he said, the kingdom of God will be taken away from such people, and given to a people who will produce its fruit.

If we are God's people, we are commanded to bear kingdom fruit. By the Spirit, "be fruitful." It is a command. It multiplies blessing. It is our desirable witness.

TWO PATHS
Genesis 5:21-24

When Enoch was 65 years old, he became the father of Methuselah. And after he had become the father of Methuselah, Enoch walked with God 300 years and had other sons and daughters. So Enoch lived a total of 365 years.

Enoch walked with God, and then he was no more, because God had taken him away.

*****

T here is much in this passage. Much that is hard to understand, but still much to be learned. Our focus is Enoch, who walked faithfully with God, and we'll explore this under three headings:

THE BACKGROUND,
THE MAN,
THE CHALLENGE.

So, we start with THE BACKGROUND.

'In the Beginning, God created the heavens and the Earth.'[27]

The opening verse of the Bible makes clear to us that we are to appreciate two dynamics of God's created order – that which is earthly and that which is heavenly. It is a concise summary of every verse which follows. As we read the biblical record, we come to see that the challenge to overcome the things of Earth in favour of the heavenly, shapes the lives of every Bible character. The same is true in the lives of all Christians throughout history.

This vast distinction between two opposing facets of God's creation not only introduces the biblical record, but also permeates through the creation account. God's creation is 'ex nihilo,' or 'Out of nothing'. God is eternal – he has always been - but the heavens and the Earth are not. So, creation week separates a time when there was nothing made, from a time when there was something made. And in each day of creation God establishes separation. Five times this word is written into the first four days of creation.

Day 1. God said, "Let there be light," and there was light. God saw that it was good and He *separated* light from darkness.[28]

Day 2. God said, "Let there be a vault between the waters, to *separate* water from water." So God made the vault and *separated* the water under the vault from the water above it.[29]

Day 3. The word 'separation' is not used, but God gathers the waters, and separates land from sea. God also commands seed bearing plants to only produce seeds according to their kind, so to remain distinguished, or separate, from other kinds.

On day 4, God said, "Let there be lights in the vault of the sky to *separate* the day from the night, and let them serve as signs to mark sacred times and days and years"... God set them in the vault of the sky to give light on Earth, to govern the day and the night, and to *separate* light from darkness.[30]

On days five and six, the living creatures received the same command to reproduce according to their kind.

God separated creation into seven individual days. He separated work from rest, sacred times from common, man from beast, male from female. Separation is everywhere in the account of creation and firmly establishes the principle that God separates one from another. It is no insignificant thing that God's first action was to separate light from darkness and, by introducing a Sabbath, his last action was to separate Holy from unholy.

Separation is also repeatedly used throughout the rest of Genesis, highlighting two divergent paths. Lot and Abram Separate - one towards the promised land; the other towards Soddom.[31] Jacob and Esau were to become two peoples whom the Lord said he would separate, one to serve the other.[32] And Jacob separated his master's flocks to produce for himself a vast and strong flock, leaving his master the weak and diminished flock.[33] So, we observe that the temporary events of Earth represent eternal heavenly truths - one promised land, one godless land; one to rule, one to serve; one spotless flock, one blemished.

Whilst Adam and Eve were both punished and withdrawn from Eden, they remained in God's presence, and united with each other. It is not until Cain and Abel that we see the root of separation amongst people, and a distinction made between those who remain in God's presence and those who do not. We read about God preferring Abel's offering over Cain's and, as a consequence of Cain's response, the Bible records the world's first murder and first occasion where God pronounces a *curse* over a man.

God asked Cain,

> *"What have you done? Listen, your brother's blood cries out to me from the ground. Now, you are under a curse."*[34]

And Cain reveals what that means when he replies,

> *"Today you are driving me from the land, and I will be hidden from your presence."*

The curse separates man from God's presence, and births two separate and contrasting genealogies - one line favoured by God; the other hidden from his presence.

Genesis 4:17-24 details Cain's family line and the moral deterioration that had occurred within seven generations of Adam. Whilst Cain was distraught at being driven from God's presence for murder, his descendant Lamech stands boastful for killing a man. The text then moves to the line of Adam through Seth, but not before Eve's pivotal declaration,

"God has granted me another child in place of Abel, since Cain killed him"[35]

This statement intentionally highlights two things,

1. Seth now stands in place of Abel, on whom the Lord looked with favour (4:4), and
2. Abel was killed by Cain, who was then cursed for the murder.

The separation between the cursed and favoured lines is highlighted and affirmed. This distinction between the two family lines is further clarified by the next verse, which tells us that at the time of Seth's son Enosh, people began to call on the name of the Lord.

In Chapter 5, we are reminded that God made mankind in his likeness (v1), and that he blessed them (v2). We are told that Seth was a son in Adam's own likeness (v3). There is no curse upon Adam or Seth, and so we read a very different account in Seth's family line. It is within this genealogy we find our young man Enoch who is twice declared to have 'walked faithfully with God.' He was then taken away by God only a third way through his anticipated life-span.

Both Enoch and Lamech were seventh from Adam - Lamech through the line of Cain, and Enoch through the line of Seth. The number 7 in the bible holds great significance for being the perfect number, symbolising completeness. If Lamech was seventh in Cain's cursed lineage, then he can be said to represent the pinnacle of ungodly living. Enoch in contrast, seventh in the favoured line of Seth, can be held to represent the pinnacle of Godly living.

From Enoch's offspring eventually comes Noah, whom God used to bring about the ultimate separation between the Godly few, and those who walked away from God toward destruction. Seth's line truly carries God's favour. To further highlight the distinction between the two lines, we read of a second Lamech, Grandson of Enoch, and Father of Noah. This Lamech of Seth's line, possesses a very different spirit to the Lamech of Cain's line. He names his child Noah, saying, "He will comfort us in the labour and painful toil of our hands caused by the ground the Lord has cursed." Whilst he laments over the painful toil of working the cursed ground, to Lamech of the favoured line, God is still 'Lord.'

The Bible sets out the ages of all these early descendants of Adam and, by doing the maths, we find that everyone in Seth's favoured line died before the flood. This gives support to the notion that this family line remained in God's favour, and none of them were killed in God's global judgement upon the godless. The flood is, of course, an event that foreshadows the ultimate global judgement of God at the second coming of Christ. This distinction between favoured and cursed runs through the pages of the entire Bible, continuing to this very day, and even to the end of the age.

In reading Genesis, one cannot escape the many links to the eternal truth that there are two separate paths in this life – one pointing towards God, and the other, away from him. There is a separation between that which is preserved, and that which is marked for destruction; those who are marked for his flock, and those who will be separated off; those whom God will reward, and those who will suffer punishment.

Now to focus our attention on THE MAN Enoch.

It is a good rule when reading a family line or genealogy in the bible to not simply skim read or bypass it, but to carefully look for any patterns and, notably, any breaks in them. These anomalies can be particularly educational. In the genealogies of Genesis

5, there is a pattern by which a man lived a certain number of years, had a son, lived a number of years more, had other sons and daughters, lived a total of such and such years, and then died.

For example,

> When Jared lived 162 years, he became the father of Enoch. After he became the father of Enoch, Jared lived 800 years and had other sons and daughters. Altogether, Jared lived 962 years, and then he died.[36]

Now look at Enoch:

> When Enoch had lived 65 years, he became the father of Methuselah.[37]

This fits the pattern.

> After he became the father of Methuselah, Enoch walked faithfully with God 300 years and had other sons and daughters.[38]

The word 'Lived' has been replaced by 'walked faithfully with God'.

> Altogether Enoch lived a total of 365 years. Enoch walked faithfully with God; then he was no-more because God took him away.'[39]

The refrain 'and then he died,' has been replaced with 'God took Him away.'

Enoch is distinguished even amongst the blessed line of Seth as being the epitome of Godly living. In the little information we are given about Seth's line, God has determined that twice in four verses, readers of Genesis should be told that Enoch walked faithfully with him. It is of great importance to recognise that, in the summary of Enoch's life, the word 'lived' is twice replaced with the words 'walked faithfully with God.' This should immediately challenge us with the reality that there is a difference between the two. Are we merely living, or are we walking faithfully with God?

Understand this, Adam was created dead! He was made in God's image and likeness, but was formed from the dust and only became a living being when God breathed into his nostrils the breath of life. Then God blessed him. There are three parts here.

- There is being formed.
- There is being given breath.
- There is being given God's blessing.

Every human being is formed by God, and is alive only by the breath that God gives them. But do not be fooled into thinking that we automatically carry God's blessing because we are alive. The blessing is for those who walk with God. Are you merely living, or are you walking with God, in his blessing?

Hebrews 11, sheds a little more light on Enoch, providing a definition of 'walking with God,' in contrast to just living:

> By faith Enoch was taken from this life, so that he did not experience death: "He could not be found because God had taken him away." For before he was taken, he was commended as one who pleased God. And without faith it is impossible to please God, because anyone who comes to him must believe that he exists and that he rewards those who earnestly seek him.

Oh, that by God's grace, the same will be said of our lives. Enoch was seventh from Adam and the perfect representation of Godly living. For 300 years, he walked with God, in faith, believing that God existed, and he did earnestly seek him. Then Enoch was taken away. It is hard for us to understand that Enoch did not die. We will come to this in a moment.

First we must comment on the years that he lived - 365 years - and the years of all those in his family line. The oldest living man on record, Methuselah, lived 969 years. This is completely alien to us. It is a cause for many to believe that the years are not literal and, at best, merely symbolic. I have found myself reading this account as I would a fictional story, impressed by the content, yet failing to connect with the fact that upon this very Earth our earliest ancestors lived for almost 1000 years!

Now, when God created mankind he filled them with his own eternal breath. They were designed to *never* experience death. Death came to them through sin, and the lifespan of mankind was reduced to only hundreds of years, which is actually *infinitely small* in comparison to an eternal lifespan. Enoch's 365 years, makes him less than middle age at the time when God took him away. Today's equivalent is someone dying in their early forties. So what is the significance of age?

In Proverbs 3:2 Solomon writes,

> *"My son, do not forget my teaching, but keep my commands in your heart, for they will prolong your life many years."*

Or, put another way, be wise and you will live longer. Long life is a desirable thing. But, as Enoch is taken by God many hundreds of years before his expected lifespan, we are reminded that long life is not our highest calling. Walking closely with God is our highest calling. Living in nearness to God far surpasses the achievement of a long life on this earth.

Besides which, remember the lament of favoured Lamech, who

longed for relief from the painful toil of life? We retire at 65. For Enoch, being retired at 365 may well have been a great mercy given him for his faithfulness.

Either way,

> *"better is one day in your courts [Lord] than a thousand elsewhere."[40]*

Enoch's life was not cut short in this age, rather it was given an extension in the next. He temporarily lived his life on Earth in the manner which he continued to live out in heaven. He walked Faithfully with God 300 years. Then God took him away.

Only two people in the Bible did not experience death, Enoch and Elijah. This is a mystery, and the Bible does contain mysteries that we need to accept in faith. Though we may not find definitive answers, we can still trust the Holy Spirit to teach us from them – even if it is just to reassert that God is too lofty for us to ever understand. We persevere with study, praying for insight.

Because of Adam's sin, God says to him, "for dust you are, and to dust you will return." Could it be considered that, such was the extent of the Godliness of Enoch and Elijah permeating through every part of their being, that there was none left of the earthly man to give back to the earth when they were taken? Such was God's work in their life, and the nearness of their walk with him, that there was nothing more to prepare or be thrown off when he took them away? No worldly nature left for the earth to repossess?

Enoch was the epitome of Godly living. So long had he walked with God, that at 365 years old his next step was perhaps naturally upwards. Such was Elijah's walk with God that his spirit was desired by Elisha, and pronounced over John the Baptist by the Angel of the Lord.

Now, I can't understand what it is to be the type of man that is received into heaven without dying, or to have my spirit pronounced over another persons life. Yet, as you read the accounts of Elijah there is such a sense of his unworldly nature that you do wonder what there was in him that needed to be returned to the earth when God took him up to heaven.

The Bible asserts that those who earnestly seek God are being transformed from one degree of glory into another. Perhaps these men reached the end of that journey before their earthly bodies succumbed to a natural death. Either way, the Spirit need not prompt us too hard to consider that these examples of Godly men are to challenge our own conduct. They are examples of men that we should desire to imitate; to call on God to shape us toward a similar status, believing it is achievable. After all, Elijah was a man just like us![41]

Of course Jesus was also ascended into heaven, but not before experiencing death. This was, after all, the ultimate purpose of his incarnate ministry – to die in place of his followers. But even then the earth did not receive his body back because he rose from death and ascended into heaven also. Echoes of the created order are sounded when, before his ascension, Jesus pronounces a blessing over his disciples - as God had over Adam and Eve - and breathed on them that life giving breath, the Holy Spirit. The original created order is echoed in the life of everyone who turns to Christ. Christians are recreated, given the breath of the Spirit, and blessed and equipped to live in God's presence.

Jesus is, of course, distinguished from Enoch and Elijah by the fact that he is God. Yet by also being fully man, Jesus, with Enoch and Elijah, are the examples of the fulfilment of our potential to live perfectly Christ-like lives, as those remade in God's image. And we are called to be perfect as the Father is perfect.[42]

> so what kind of people ought you to be? You ought to live Holy and Godly lives.[43]

Holy and Godly. Not good. Not better than a few you could name. Not earthly. Perfect. Holy. Godly. That which is Godly will remain, that which is earthly will be abandoned back to the earth.

> *Put to death, therefore, whatever belongs to your earthly nature... since you have taken off your old self with its practices and have put on the new self, which is being renewed in knowledge in the image of its Creator.[44]*

A final word on Enoch. He is quoted in Jude, a book which reflects upon the two ways of living that we've looked at. The quote itself comes from the apocryphal 'book of Enoch', and though this book has not come to be regarded as part of the canon of scripture, this quote has been included in the Bible, and so should be considered as authoritative.

> *"See, the Lord is coming with thousands upon thousands of his holy ones to judge everyone, and to convict all of them of all the ungodly acts they have committed in their ungodliness, and of all the defiant words ungodly sinners have spoken against him."[45]*

This verse comes after Jude's own comment,

> *Woe to them who have taken the way of Cain.[46]*

We have been brought right back, then, to the two family lines, the two paths to choose between.

And so, to THE CHALLENGE.

Listen to this. There is the line of Cain, and there is the line of Seth. Two paths, and only two. One blessed; one cursed. One earthly;

one Godly. One is life; one is death. And there is no middle road. Our choice is not a future event. We have already chosen. Right now we stand on one or the other, and our ongoing choice is whether or not we stay on the path we have chosen, or abandon it and move to the other.

After Jude's letter, comes the book of Revelation. Hear the words of Chapter 3:14-18.

> *"These are the words of the Amen, the faithful and true witness, the ruler of God's creation. I know your deeds, that you are neither hot nor cold. I wish you were either one or the other! So, because you are lukewarm - neither hot nor cold - I am about to spit you out of my mouth."*

Those who are Luke warm, will be spat out of God's mouth for being neither hot nor cold. Lukewarm is not merely the state of being neither cold nor hot, but it is in fact both together. A tap only produces lukewarm water, when hot and cold run together.

Are you hot and cold? Are you one who holds out your tithe, but fails to hold back your tongue? Do you hold a Bible, and hold a grudge as well? Are you one who rushes to be filled with the Holy Spirit, but becomes drunk on alcohol? Do you give time to God, but ignore the needy? Pursue a relationship with God, and also with the world? Do you accept praise, but despise correction? Do you fear God, but also fear man?

> *God is light; in him there is no darkness at all. If we claim to have fellowship with him and yet walk in the darkness, we lie and do not live out the truth.[47]*

Why would God wish you were one or the other? For God to destroy what is completely opposed to him is bad enough, for he loves everyone and gives everyone the chance to turn to him.

How then must it be for him to destroy those who show signs of allegiance, and yet fail to fully abandon their earthliness? They are hot and cold together, and he spits them out.

When Jesus called his disciples, he said, "come and follow me." There was no in-between. They either followed him or they didn't. Staying where they were was the same as walking away. They either walked with him or against him. The same is true of us. We walk with Jesus, or against him.

> *Do not protect that area in your life that you know is contrary to God's word. Protect your life. Do not for a moment entertain that godless practice. Instead be resilient and live.*
>
> *If we walk in the light, as he is in the light, we have fellowship with one another, and the blood of Jesus, his Son, purifies us from all sin.[48]*

For those currently lukewarm, there is hope. In Revelation 3, God continues by saying,

> *"Those whom I love, I rebuke and discipline, so be earnest and repent. Here I am, I stand at the door and knock. If anyone hears my voice and opens the door, I will come in and eat with that person."*

God is trying to make himself heard by you. Listen. Then make your choice. God's discipline awaits anyone who leaves the path, and thank God it does because:

> *the one who hates correction will die.[49]*

Accept his loving rebuke, repent and live; or refuse it and die. Receive God's love and blessing, or his curse.

For those who have not yet come to know Christ as their saviour, there is hope too. But you must understand that, now you have heard of these two paths, you are without excuse.

Listen,

> *All have sinned and fall short of the glory of God.[50]*

None of us are, by nature, perfect. But we are either walking the way of Seth, reliant on God and offering ourselves to his ongoing work of changing us from one degree of glory to the next; or we are walking the way of Cain, becoming more and more indifferent and enslaved by our sinfulness, heading towards destruction. If you know of the sin in your life and are content for it to go unaddressed, then woe to you who have taken the way of Cain. Too long on this road, and your indifference will walk you right into the fire.

But, what say you, man who has chosen the path of life?

> *The Lord is my shepherd, He guides me along the right paths*
> *for His name's sake.[51]*

May he keep me on the right path. Brothers, remain humble and allow him to achieve his good works in and through you. Wait on the Lord and renew your strength, run and do not grow weary, walk and do not faint.

> *"Be very careful to keep the commandment and the law that*
> *Moses the servant of the Lord gave you: to love the Lord your*
> *God, to walk in obedience to him, to keep his commands, to*
> *hold fast to him and to serve him with all your heart and*
> *with all your soul."[52]*

There are two paths. Only two. Give careful thought to the paths for your feet.

And to close. Consider your unbelieving friends; family; colleagues. What path do they tread? How does this message effect the way you pray for the lost? Do not pray as if a time will come about for them to choose... pray earnestly for the choice that they have *already* made, that they might be turned around.

Those who do not believe in Christ's salvation are not stood still needing to make a choice which way to walk, rather with every day they are walking further down the path of Cain. Salvation is on offer for all who truly repent, however far they've travelled down the wrong path.

To the unbeliever: Salvation is available to you, to give you life.
To the Lukewarm: Restoration is available to you, to put you back on the right path.
To the believer: strength is available to you, to persevere on the path of life.

Two paths: A theme running throughout scripture:

Will you keep to the old path that the wicked have trod? (Job 22:15)

There are those who rebel against the light, who do not know its ways or stay in its paths (Job 24:13)

[The Lord] prepared a path for his anger; he did not spare them from death but gave them over to the plague (Psalms 78:50)

but you [Lord] make known to me the path of life (Psalms 16:11)

Direct me in the path of your commands, for there I find delight (Psalms 119:35)

I run in the path of your commands, for you have broadened my understanding (Psalms 119:32)

I gain understanding from your precepts; therefore I hate every wrong path (Psalms 119:104)

Blessed is the one who does not walk in step with the wicked (Psalm 1:1)

my son, do not go along with them, do not set foot on their paths (Proverbs 1:15)

thus you will walk in the ways of the good, and keep to the paths of the righteous (Proverbs 2:20)

in all you ways submit to him, and he will make your paths straight (Proverbs 3:6)

Give careful thought to the paths for your feet and be steadfast in all your ways (Proverbs 4:26)

for your ways are in full view of the Lord, and he examines your paths (Proverbs 5:21)

Whoever strays from the path of the prudent comes to rest in the company of the dead (Proverbs 21:26)

You [Lord] have made known to me the paths of life; you will fill me with Joy in your presence (Acts 2:28)

Walk by the Spirit, and you will not gratify the desires of the flesh (Galations 5:16)

Keep in step with the Spirit (Galatians 5:25)

Walk faithfully (Genesis 5)

TAKE GOD AT HIS WORD, OR
TAKE RESPONSIBIILITY

Genesis16:1-2

Now Sarai, Abram's wife, had borne him no children. But she had an Egyptian slave named Hagar; so she said to Abram, "The Lord has kept me from having children. Go, sleep with my slave; perhaps I can build a family through her."[53]

*****

My wife and I like to watch films. We have come to notice that, in any action film we have seen, if ever any person comes to discover a bomb, they have one of two reactions. And their reactions are largely due to a relatively small part - the timer.

If there are several hours on the display, then people generally remain fairly calm. They are thoughtful in their actions - backing away slowly, ringing for support and evacuating in an orderly fashion. Contrast that to when the timer shows less than a minute. You can imagine the scene as people react on instinct and fear.

In recent history, we have been reminded that deadly explosives are not just a thing of fictional films. Time and again the world has had to react to the reality of the situation. Bombs and mass killings, and supposedly in the name of religion. The world is regularly caused to grieve in the wake of such atrocities, and try to understand why and how these events could ever happen. Thoughts quickly turn to, "Where is God in this? Why is this allowed to happen?" We start to look at *all* the atrocities that have happened throughout history and ask,

"God, where were you in this?"

Well, God is right there throughout history making promises to bless those who are faithful to him. Promises to love them, prosper them, build them up, draw them to himself. And yet, through mankind's unfaithfulness and lack of trust in his words; people's decisions to take matters into their own hands; mankind turns its back on God. Man walks away from him and then has the audacity to ask where *he* was.

It happens time and time again since the very first man, Adam. Yet God remains faithful to his promise to bless those who will return to him and live according to his rule. He faithfully welcomes and blesses all who truly repent.

The account of Abram and Sarai, and their challenge to claim God's promises, draws this out very well. It projects this over each of our lives:

Take God at his word, or be prepared to take responsibility.

Setting the scene: Looking at God's promise to Abram.

In Genesis 12, Abram is the recipient of a very elaborate promise. God promises him:

"I will make you into a great nation, and I will bless you;

I will make your name great,
so that you will be a blessing.
I will bless those who bless you
and curse those who curse you;
and all the families of the earth
will be blessed through you."

Abram, one man, will become a mighty nation. All people's on earth will be blessed by him. And, how a man shall act towards Abram, God shall act towards them. An elaborate promise indeed. The promise to become a great nation is especially notable when you consider what is revealed of his wife Sarai in the previous chapter. Genesis 11:30 says:

> *Sarai was childless because she was unable to conceive.*

The bible very clearly establishes Sarai's inability to bear children *before* we read about God's promise to make Abram a great nation. From the offset, Abram is called to believe God's word to do the impossible, and shake off all his experience and evidence to the contrary.

Abram's timing.

Now, when God gave Abram this promise, it seems that Abram took the promise and attached one of those little timers to it. When God promises to make a great nation from him, Abram heard a little stipulation that wasn't there. And its based on timing. It goes like this,

> *'I will make you into a great nation. I will do this by giving you a son... before Sarai is beyond the supposed age of childbearing.'*

And so, whether consciously or not, Abram set a countdown and affixed it to God's promise. By chapter 15, the countdown had all but run to zero. The problem with setting our own time-frames and interpretation for God's promises is that as time starts running out, so does our faith. The more time that expires since God's promise to Abram, the more he seems to doubt God.

If we're honest, we all tend to do this with God's promises. There are endless ways in which we can do this, but all of them seem to involve putting words in God's mouth and setting our own time-frame. They all lead to the same type of response that Abram's has to God's word. When God says to Abram,

> *"Do not be afraid Abram. I am your shield, your very great reward,"[54]*

Abram responds,

> *"what can you give me since I remain childless? ...You have given me no children; so a servant in my household will be my heir."[55]*

Now we immediately start to see the problems we have in waiting for God's promises - those little seeds of doubt that get sown and grow as time goes by. By Genesis 16, those seeds have grown sufficiently in Abram and Sarai, to lead them to question God's faithfulness and ability to fulfil his word. Three striking dangers are revealed in Abram's questions.

> *"What can you give me, since I remain childless?"*

Firstly, Abram questions what God can give him? What he can actually do? Abram reminds God that he has not yet come through on his last promise. In his mind, so much time had passed without God producing a son, that he is now reviewing all of God's words in light of the fact that the first promise is yet unfulfilled.

There's another perhaps more troubling element to this question. God says, "I am your reward." but Abram misses this. His reply is "What can you give me?". Abram has lost perspective; he is asking about what earthly things God can give him, when the Lord and creator of all things is offering his very self! Because Abram has not trusted God with the first promise and the timing of its fulfil ment, God himself is not enough for Abram! So easy it is to make our relationship with God of lesser importance than what earthly things we may get out of it.

Danger number two. "I remain childless...You have given me no children." Two references to what God hasn't done, revealing a despondency - even hostility - towards God. It can be entirely correct and edifying to remind God of his promises to us. This can be evidence of our faith. It is quite another thing to be downcast and even angry towards God because we haven't seen his promise fulfilled within our desired time-fame. These are the products of our doubt.

And thirdly,

> "the one who will inherit my estate is Eliezer of Damascus.... a servant in my household will be my heir."

God has not come through for Abram in his own time-frame, so not only does he question God's ability to come through for him, he is now telling God what will happen in the future! In his mind, Abram has determined the events to come. He not only doubts God, but puts himself in God's place!

How often do we question God because he hasn't acted soon enough? How often do we doubt God's provision? How often do we prefer earthly things, when the heavenly is on offer? How often is our reaction to God based upon what we think we know about the future? For me, far too much!

Now, God is gracious. He is slow to anger over Abram's doubt, and quick to respond in love. He gently takes Abram outside his tent and shows him the infinite stars hanging from the heavens, saying,

> "Look up at the sky and count the stars - if indeed you can count them... so shall your offspring be."[56]

It is as if God was saying, "You want something physical as proof of my faithfulness? Here is a nightly reminder of what I can do!" Abram believed God and it was credited it to him as righteousness. So Abram's hope is restored and his faith renewed.... for a time.

In his grace, God gave Abram and Sarai the stars to look at as a reminder of his word. Yet, as time passed by, doubt creeps in again. What God had given as a reminder of his favour, perhaps may have started to become a reminder of his apparent lack of action. As each night passed, those stars must have been harder and harder to look at; a constant reminder of the absence of the child they were so excited over.

How easy it is to allow doubt to pervert those blessings and graces of God. To listen to that ancient serpent still whispering, "Did God *really* say....? God's own words get twisted into accusation; into that which we hold against him. How easy to allow doubt to creep in, and turn our faith into indifference and even anger towards God. And so often, it is all based upon timing.

And so we reach Genesis 16:2, the day that the countdown has reached zero. Abram and Sarai had both been well aware that Sarai could not bear children, and they had waited until Abram was 86 before they started looking for alternative ways to start this great nation that God had promised. Would we be so patient?

Imagine, if you can, how many hours were spent throughout the years, pondering when God would come through on his promises? Or, if they had even heard him correctly? How many nights they sat together under the very stars God told Abram to count, praying and weeping and begging God to give them the promised child? How many years that disappointment gradually withered away their expectancy and faith? Perhaps We can relate to this? The day came when they started looking for their own answers. Perhaps we can relate to this too?

Worldly means.

> *Now Sarai, Abram's wife, had borne him no children. But*
> *she had an Egyptian slave named Hagar; so she said to*
> *Abram, "The Lord has kept me from having children. Go*
> *sleep with my slave; perhaps I can build a family through*
> *her." Abram agreed to what Sarai said.[57]*

Guys, be accountable to someone. Married couples, have someone outside your marriage to be accountable to. Sarai was weak
in offering Hagar to Abram. Abram was weak in accepting the
offer. They were both weak, having endured years of suffering the
same issue. There's no record of a single word of prayer on their
decision, they just acted. Even if you're married, find someone
you trust and be accountable to them. It will pay dividends at
times when you are weak, to have someone who will listen, pray
for you, and hold you to prayer also.

And so, in verse 3, we read that Abram took Sarai's Egyptian slave
Hagar in place of his own wife. Our ears might well prick up when
we hear the word 'Egyptian.' It is a detail that the Bible is spe-
cific to point out, and an important one. Throughout the biblical
record Egypt becomes an analogy of bondage and slavery to this
world, in opposition to freedom and faith in God. It is first mentioned in the Bible when Abram travelled there to outlive the
famine God sent to Canaan.

Rather than staying in the promised land, trusting God for provision, Abram begins this pattern of trusting in worldly resources
instead. Stay in the land God promised him? or go down to Egypt
where they still had plenty of food? Live in God's promise? Or
make your own way? The same choice is later given to his promised son Isaac during another famine, but God gives him clear instruction on the matter,

"Do not go down to Egypt; live in the land where I tell you to live. Stay in this land for a while, and I will be with you and will bless you."[58]

When Gen 16:3 mentions Hagar as Sarai's Egyptian slave, it is stressing the reoccurring theme of choosing between what God has promised and what this world can offer. Abram slept with Hagar, and she conceived.

If ever we fail to persevere in trusting God's eternal perspective, it is often the case that we have neglected to look all that far ahead. With one impulsive suggestion, Sarai has set for herself a life of jealousy, resentment and strife. Not just between herself and Hagar, but between her and her husband. Imagine the situation. Sarai, who is unable to conceive, offers her slave to her husband. Hagar is still Sarai's servant, but is also joined to her husband and bearing his child. And Sarai's servant, pregnant by her husband, now begins to despise her.

What's Sarai's response? She goes to accuse her husband, saying,

"You are responsible for the wrong that I am suffering.... May God judge between you and me."

The union through which God chose to bless all nations, has become polluted with accusation and division. And it all goes from very bad to worse. Abram wipes his hands of the situation, Sarai mistreats Hagar, and Hagar and her son are forced to flee. Abram and Sarai are much worse off than before. They are still childless and, instead of gaining a son, Abram loses one. Their lack of faith has instead produced loss, resentment, blame and mistrust.

These are but a few of the fruits of neglecting faith in God for the preference of worldly attitudes and resources; of trying to snatch after worldly pleasure, or even what God has promised, instead of throwing away the timer and standing firm in faith.

Butterfly effect.

You have perhaps heard of the butterfly effect, where the beating of a butterfly's wings on one side of the world has a ripple effect which results in an earthquake on the other. Preferring our own agendas over God's it not only detrimental to our own lives, it can sow the seeds for a bad harvest all around, and for generations to come.

Stepping back into today's world, our news is plastered with the horrific atrocities that are being carried out by ISIS, and the like. This world is being ravished and millions of people's lives devastated by the actions of an extremist sect of the Islamic faith. It is from Ishmael's second son Kedar, that Islam's prophet Mohammed was descended. Islam's key prophet was the product of the decision that Abram and Sarai made to go ahead of God and act according to their own agenda; a descendant of Abram's son through Hagar.

Islamic tradition holds Ishmael, not Isaac, to be the child that God required Abram to sacrifice, and Muslims believe that the fulfilment of God's promise to bless all nations comes through him. God does say that Hagar's descendants will also be too numerous to count, but look at what the Bible says was promised over Ishmael, when Hagar called on God:

> *He will be a wild donkey of a man; his hand will be against everyone and everyone's hand against him, and he will live in hostility toward all his brothers.[59]*

It would be overwhelmingly ignorant to suggest that all descendants of Ishmael are therefore dangerous enemies to us who inherit the promise of Abraham, through Isaac. It cannot be overlooked however that, just as God is honouring his promises to bless every nation through Isaac, so too are his promises over Ishmael echoing throughout history to this very day.

The extremist branches of Islam who do pose a very real threat to Christians, amongst many others, are the product of a lineage through Ishmael, and a promise that would never have come about if Abram and Sarai had held firm in their faith. It is a very stark and very real warning for us of the dangers of going ahead of God, or harbouring any attitudes which allow us to stray from his promises and plans for our lives.

God's will.

So we finish by looking at how we can remain faithful when God makes a promise. Look again at what God had promised Abram,

> *"Go from your country, your people,*
>
> *and your father's household*
> *I will show you the land*
> *I will make you into a great nation*
> *I will bless you*
> *I will make your name great[60]*
> *You will be a blessing*
> *I will bless those who bless you and curse those who curse you*
> *All people will be blessed through you.*
> *To your offspring I will give this land"[61]*

Let's look at the significance of these words "I will." It is not just a promise to do something, it is a statement of God's *will.* It is God saying, "I will this to happen!". When we hear the words "I will this," or "I will that," our emphasis is usually on the 'This' and 'That,' but we need to remember to emphasise the "I will."

If we focus on the 'this' and 'that', we get discouraged when it doesn't appear in our preferred time frame. If we remember the "I will" bit, and we put our faith in the fact that it is God's will and promise, our faith is set on firm foundations. We more naturally hand the timing of the fulfilment to him.

The world likes to tell us,

- There's no time like the present.
- It's about time!
- Time waits for no man.
- Time is slipping away.

Let me encourage you, time is certainly not slipping away! For a Christian living with an eternal heavenly perspective, time is not running out. Now, there is certainly a significance in timing. We do only have one allocated time span within which to contend with this earthly body. A person whom has not yet accepted Jesus as saviour has only a certain time-frame within which they can respond to the good news of the gospel, and so determine their eternal destiny.

But Christians can easily hold too firmly to a worldly perspective when it comes to time. Consider the song Amazing Grace:

> When we've been there 10,000 years,
> bright shining as the sun,
> We've no less days to sing God's praise,
> as when we first begun.

When we've been there 10,000 years.... 10,000 years! with no less still to come! Is time running out? I think that after 10,000 years we may look back with amusement at when we were tempted to lose faith because God took 1, 2, 5, 10, 50 years to fulfil one of his promises to us. "50 years," we might chuckle! "P'ah, 50 years! I was so spiritually immature back then. What is 50 years between my creator and me, when he has established a relationship with me that spans eternity?"

And let me pick up that idea that God may have taken 50 years to fulfil ONE of his promises to you or me. Let us not forget that God fulfils promises to us every day.

> I will not leave you, nor forsake you[62]

It is spiritual immaturity to resent God for the time he has determined to fulfil one promise in our own time-frame, when he is proving his ongoing faithfulness to us on a daily basis. He has given us our own stars to look at daily, to remind us of his faithfulness when we struggle to trust him for promises as yet unfulfilled.

Those promises of God that you and I are waiting for, those are not the end results of our faith, they are not the end game. They are but tiny brushstrokes upon the eternal picture of God's glory. The end result of your faith is that praise, glory and honour be given when Christ Jesus is revealed, and your souls saved from God's wrath. Our faith is tested in temporary matters, so that it is built up and proven genuine when Christ is revealed.

For those Christians who have been battling with God over promises thus far unfulfilled; for those who have found that time has allowed worldly attitudes to creep in, and seeds of doubt to grow: make the opportunity to have God dig that out of you from the root. Submit yourself again to God's will, and God's timing, and God's peace! Trust that your patience is being rewarded by bringing glory to God, and by the maturing of your faith.

> The world and its desires pass away, but whoever does the will of God lasts forever.[63]

> "For I know the plans I have for you," declares the Lord, "plans to prosper you and not to harm you, plans to give you a hope and a future."[64]

So we finish with another verse of Amazing Grace, and I wonder how much of it was inspired by God's promise to Abram?

> The Lord has promised good to me,
> His word my hope secures.
> He will my shield and portion be,
> as long as life endures.

THE MESSENGER
Malachi 3:1

"I will send my messenger, who will prepare the way before me. Then suddenly the Lord you are seeking will come to his temple; the messenger of the covenant, who you desire, will come" says the Lord Almighty."[65]

*****

Malachi 3 is about a Messenger - the messenger of the covenant, who will come and make things right with God's people. We live in a time when we await the second coming of Christ. In Malachi's time people are, of course, still waiting for his first coming. They are eagerly looking ahead to when this messenger of the covenant will arrive. And in this passage God says through Malachi, 'The messenger is coming, be ready.'

We're going to look at this message in the context of the entire Bible; in the context of the people of Malachi's time; for its relevance to Christians today; and for its relevance to the contemporary world in which we live.

The Message in the context of the entire Bible.

God's plan throughout the Bible is like the workings of a huge distillery - purifying and separating his people throughout history. Generation after generation are poured into it, and God is at work purifying those who are his, by separating them from uncleanliness.

At creation, God created light and saw it was good. He separated it from darkness. Revelation describes the separation of the final judgement. The Bible begins with God dwelling with his perfect man in Eden, and it finishes with God dwelling amongst perfect men in the new Jerusalem. All the pages in between are centred on a covenant relationship between God and man:

"I will be your God, and you will be my people."[66]

God has always honoured this covenant, and is patiently enduring the task of bringing his people back in line with it. But there will come a time when those who have hardened their hearts will be removed for good, whilst those who are found faithful will be received to dwell with him forever. Indeed Malachi 3:18 says,

"And you will again see the distinction between the righteous and the wicked."

The theme of Malachi is this: The great King will come not only to judge his people, but also to bless and restore them. So, we do not need to be anxious about judgement if we are those belonging to God. But we must respond to the need of wholly aligning ourselves with him. God is warning his people. But what is the purpose of the warning?

"I have sent this warning so that my covenant with Levi will continue...

A covenant of life and peace."[67]

This covenant is repeatedly referenced throughout Malachi, and it is the same one that we are in today, though now we fulfil our part through Jesus.

The Message in the context of the people of Malachi's time

Israel had returned to Jerusalem from exile in Babylon. They had their new temple but, over time, the priests had become corrupt and the people intermarried with foreigners, ignored the Sabbath and tithing, and offered defective animals as sacrifices to God. Sacrifices were a burden to them, and the offering of blemished animals instead of acceptable offerings had brought a curse on them. They violated the covenant, and it brought them humiliation.

So, they weep on the alter because God does not look on them with favour, but God does not look on them with favour because they offer lame sacrifices. It is a vicious circle and something's got to change. Since God does not change,[68] the situation requires God's people to. This is the purpose of God's message to them through Malachi, and as we explore this passage we must be mindful that the same message applies to us.

> *"I will send my messenger, who will prepare the way before me."*

This was John the Baptist.

> *"Then suddenly the Lord you are seeking will come to his temple; the messenger of the covenant whom you desire..... will come, says the Lord Almighty."*

Now, a coin has two sides. There will come a day when the King of Kings shall return to pronounce his verdict. At Jesus' first coming, he brought close to himself those who received him wholeheartedly, and he vehemently divided off those merely paying him lip service; speaking God's name but rejecting his living Word. The phrase, 'be careful what you wish for' comes to mind. When you cry out, 'Come, Lord,' be sure that he will like what he sees.

"Be on your guard to not be unfaithful."[69]

Who can endure the day of his coming? Who can stand when he appears?[70]

Two questions intended to emphasise the point: Check yourself that you are in good standing with the Lord.

For he will be like a refiners fire, or a launderer's soap. He will sit as a refiner and purifier of silver.[71]

It is very easy to imagine that we can casually come into the presence of Jesus, who will gently wash away our sins, our dirt, only to then leave him and go play in the mud between washes. It is easy for us to pay Jesus lip service on a Sunday, asking him to come and cleanse us, and then to resume living as we had before: reaching for that extra glass; telling those little lies; watching that show; clicking that link; speaking about that person; leaving that anger or unforgiveness unchecked. We then presume to return to church on Sunday for a blessing! Ultimately, we are presenting God a blemished offering.

I urge you, brothers and sisters, in view of God's mercy, to offer your bodies as a living sacrifice, holy and pleasing to God--this is your true and proper worship.[72]

This is not a message of cheap grace, this is a message of God scrubbing and burning out the impurities that have stained his church. If your heart is in breach of the covenant, it will be revealed when you stand trial. The impurities will be removed by fire.

He will purify the Levites and refine them like gold and silver. Then the Lord will have men who will bring offerings in righteousness.[73]

Now, God does not change. He has never forsaken his covenant nor his people. Even when the majority of his people have abandoned it, he has always remained true to those faithful few who uphold it. The covenant still stands because of God's faithfulness, and he has always implored people to return to it.

Every trial that the Israelites faced in the Bible was as a result of them breaking the covenant. God always pre-warned them and, though they turned away, he used their trials as discipline and reached out to them to return once again to himself. There was always a remnant who kept faith with God, and so the process was ever refining his people. Malachi 3:7 is God's message to the Israelites, and it is his message to everyone throughout history,

"Return to me, and I will return to you."

The Relevance for Christians today.

There is light and there is darkness. There are those in the dark, who do need to be fearful of judgement, and there are those who are coming into the light, living by the truth. This is not a case of perfect or imperfect by our own merits, it is a case of belonging to Jesus, or not. Christians would do well to consider the following questions:

- Is our faith in Jesus, or not?
- Do we live fully submitted to Jesus, or do we live for ourselves?
- Are we just listening, or obeying?
- Are we just turning up at church, or being the church?
- Are we simply leaning on our faith, or driving it forward?

- Are we merely 'talking Christian,' or 'living Christian?'
- Are we speaking the words, or following The Word?
- Are we dragging God along behind us, or letting him lead.

The pastor of a church I used to attend, offered me this insight: "it is usually those who love God, who are most unsettled by the challenge of such questions, and those who need it the most, who don't hear it." If we can stand the test, its only by the conviction, discipline and power of Jesus himself. We can't do a thing to please God by our own efforts, but we can do all things through Christ who strengthens us.[74]

> *Therefore if anyone is in Christ, he is a new creature; the old things have passed away; behold, new things have come. [75]*

> *Do not conform to the pattern of this world, but be transformed by the renewing of your mind.[76]*

Brothers and sisters, don't present yourself as a lame offering, but in Christ, present yourself as a holy and pleasing sacrifice.

The relevance for our world.

The Levites were offering lame sacrifices. Malachi 3:8 says that the people were robbing God by not offering the whole tithe. God isn't saying this merely to condemn, but to lead people to repentance and his blessing for obedience. God tells them to bring the full tithe. He says,

> *"Test me in this. See if I will not throw open the floodgates of heaven and pour out so much blessing that there will not be enough room to store it."[77]*

This is not a prosperity gospel. This is a test of faithfulness by which a man's heart is revealed, and which allows God to generously bless those who obey him. And the blessing that comes when God's people return to a right standing with him, is a witness to the nations. They will see the delightful land of God's people and call them blessed.

What of today's world? Which nation can we look at today and call it blessed? Is ours? Can we look upon our own nation, which legalises things that God forbids? Which gives everyone a voice, but tries to silence the undiluted gospel? Do we think that we as a nation can stand on the day of his coming? The most prosperous countries in the world have used despicable means to come to power, to maintain it, and to assert it on others. Britain is one of those.

And so we see, God allows even ungodly nations to prosper and grow. The question to which Malachi 3 responds is,

> "where is the God of Justice?"[78]

The Israelites looked at those evil nations who were prospering around them, whilst God's own people were weeping and wailing. They cynically say,

> "All who do evil are good in the eyes of the Lord, and he is pleased with them."[79]

So we see today the growing threat to Christians from radical religious groups, regimes, and countries. Such evil enacted out upon Christians all around the world, and so often that it rarely makes the news. We might look at this rise in global persecution and ask, "where is the God of justice?" 'Why won't he bring judgement?' Be careful about what you wish for.

We might look at this world and wonder if we are entering the scenario described in Luke 21, where people are fainting from terror, apprehensive of what is coming upon us. Is this global situation that which will develop to beckon the Son of Man to finally return. The souls under the altar are told to wait until the full number of Christians have been martyred before the King returns. We don't know when that number will be reached, but the number is increasing at a rapid rate. Be sure that you are ready. Sooner or later, judgement will come to us all.

Daniel speaks of his vision of a great beast. He was told that the beast will,

> speak against the Most High and oppress his holy people and try to change the set times and the laws. The holy people will be given into his hands for a time....

> But the court will sit, and his power will be taken away and completely destroyed forever. Then the sovereignty, power and greatness of all the kingdoms under heaven will be handed over to the holy people of the Most High. His Kingdom will be an everlasting Kingdom, and all rulers will worship and obey him.[80]

> The beast will be destroyed, but the holy people of the Most High will receive the kingdom and possess it forever - yes for ever and ever.[81]

The rain falls on both the good and the evil. Even the evil prosper for a time, but God's kingdom lasts forever. Does your prosperity fool you into thinking you are on the right path? Or are you certain about your place in God's kingdom because of your faith in Jesus, the messenger of the covenant?

So, finally, an observation on this Messenger himself.

> *For God so loved the world that he gave his one and only Son, that whoever believes in him shall not perish but have eternal life. For God did not send his Son into the world to condemn the world, but to save the world through him.[82]*

Jesus is the messenger of the covenant. It is our response to Jesus that secures our salvation. During his ministry, Jesus rebuked everyone at some time or other. The Religious leaders and authorities. Even his own disciples. It was divisive, and intentionally so. Those who refused the rebuke, walked away from Jesus. They chose to reject him. Those who accepted the rebuke not only accepted Jesus, but were blessed by it because it caused them to learn and mature.

When Jesus brings a rebuke, it is the discipline of God which brings us back to the covenant and invokes God's blessing. Proverbs 12:1 says,

> *Whoever loves discipline loves knowledge, but whoever hates correction is stupid.[83]*

Do we love knowledge, or hate correction? Do we accept Jesus, or deny him? If you are anything short of confident in your redemption through the blood of Jesus Christ, then you need to act. Don't leave your defective sacrifice laid on the alter, do not be like those who cry out for God to bless them, and go on robbing him. Those of you who want to enter into a covenant relationship with God, or return once more to it, hear this:

> *anyone who comes to him must believe that he exists and that he rewards those who earnestly seek him.[84]*

Believe and be earnest.

Malachi anticipates the coming of Jesus. It is the last book and summation of the entire Old Testament, which anticipates the coming of the saviour. The very next book is Matthew, which details the genealogy, birth and ministry of Jesus. His first coming now sits over two thousand years ago, and the countdown is growing ever smaller. Let us be inspired anew to remember his second coming, and live determined to be found as one who has accepted Christ.

THE FIVE SEATS

Matthew 2: 1-12 & Luke 2: 8-18

After Jesus was born in Bethlehem in Judea, during the time of King Herod, Magi from the East came to Jerusalem and asked, "Where is the one who has been born the king of the Jews? We saw his star when it rose and have come to worship him."

When King Herod heard this he was disturbed, and all Jerusalem with him. When he had called together all the people's chief priests and teachers of the law, he asked them where the Messiah was to be born. "In Bethlehem in Judea," they replied, "for this is what the prophet has written:

"'But you, Bethlehem, in the land of Judea, are by no means least among the rulers of Judea; for out of you will come a ruler who will shepherd my people Israel.'"

Then Herod called the Magi secretly and found out from them the exact time the star had appeared. He sent them to Bethlehem and said, "Go and search carefully for the child. As soon as you find him, report to me, so that I too may go and worship him."

After they had heard the king, they went on their way, and the star they had seen when it rose went ahead of them until it stopped over the place where the child was. When they saw the star, they were overjoyed. On coming to the house, they saw the child with his mother Mary, and they bowed down and worshipped him. Then they opened their treasures and presented him with gifts of Gold, Frankincense and Myrrh. And having been warned in a dream not to go back to Herod, they returned to their country by another route.[85]

And there were shepherds living out in the fields nearby, keeping watch over their flocks at night. An angel of the

Lord appeared to them, and the glory of the Lord shone around them, and they were terrified. But the angel said to them, "Do not be afraid. I bring you great news that will bring joy to all the people. Today in the town of David a saviour has been born to you; He is the Messiah, the Lord. This will be a sign to you: you will find a Baby wrapped in cloths and Lying in a manger."

Suddenly a great company of the heavenly host appeared with the angel, praising God and saying,

"Glory to God in the highest heaven, and on earth peace to those on whom his favour rests."

When the angels had left them and gone into heaven, the shepherds said to one another, "Let's go to Bethlehem and see this thing that has happened, which the Lord has told us about."

So they hurried off and found Mary and Joseph, and the baby, who was lying in the manger. When they had seen him, they spread the word concerning what had been told them about this child, and all who heard it were amazed at what the shepherds said to them.[86]

*****

I magine that before you is placed five seats, each for a different kind of person. These five seats represent one of five characters from the nativity account. By the end of this reflection, you may find that you relate more to one than the others. I trust this will help you know how to ask God to move you forward in your faith. First, a few questions:

What does God look like?
What do you think of when we talk about God?

And what about Jesus? Who is he?
And what does he look like to you?

When we read the Gospels and look at their accounts of the birth of Jesus, we read about a small handful of very different types of people, and how they took the news about a new king being born.

In the first seat, we shall sit King Herod. Herod was King in Jerusalem at the time of Jesus' birth. He was a powerful man and did whatever it took to hold onto that power, so the idea of a new King on the block upset him terribly. He wanted to stay King, and he was prepared to kill anyone who tried to take that power from him, even his own family. To Herod, the best thing that he could have was his crown, and he did not like the idea of it being given to anyone else.

In the second seat shall sit a representative of the people of Jerusalem at the time, who were also troubled along with Herod. You see Herod might have been a highly unsavoury character, but generally there was order in Jerusalem and people knew what to expect. And with Herod's power lust and temper, a challenger might just bring a dormant but highly volatile Jerusalem to uproar.

The current rule of Jerusalem wasn't perfect but it was stable, so no-one knew what the challenge of a new king might mean, and they feared change. They may not have had the perfect sovereign, but they didn't want anyone else doing the job.

The third seat is occupied by the high priest who represented the Jewish community. The religious leaders were alarmed to hear that their King had been born, and they hadn't known about it or recognised him. You see, they were unhappy about being ruled by Herod and the Romans, and were praying for God to send the Messiah to save them. They wanted change, and were awaiting a great hero to overthrow their Roman enemy and give them back their own rule. They didn't recognise Jesus as their King because he was not what they were expecting.

A humble shepherd shall take his place in the forth seat. Shepherds were not powerful or important men. If you wanted to broadcast news of great significance, say, about the birth of a royal baby, you likely wouldn't ask a shepherd to do it! They didn't expect to be called upon by an angel to proclaim the birth of Jesus and, however excited they were about the news, they probably didn't feel worthy of the calling.

The final chair is reserved for one of the Magi. These people have travelled from a distant land to take their place in the story. They were gentiles, far removed from the Jewish nation and their claim as God's chosen people. They were not Kings or wise men as we may have come to understand them, but rather they were either a type of sorcerer, or philosopher or priest of a foreign culture; practitioners of astrology who looked to the stars for knowledge and insight. Indeed, they had seen an extraordinary star, one like no other, and believed it to mark the arrival of a similarly extraordinary King, to whom they wished to bring fine gifts and, more importantly, their worship.

They had made a long journey, expecting to find a king. It has been noted that their question was not 'Is there a King here?' but rather 'Where is he that is born King of the Jews?'. The existence of a king was unquestioned, they just enquired where he was to be found. They were acting on faith, based on the signs in creation surrounding them. There was something in them that knew there was something more, someone more, and their faith led them into action to discover him.

They were looking for a king, so it was reasonable to assume that the palace would have some answers. Can you imagine what they thought when the star directed them to a stable? An extraordinary king perhaps, but certainly not one recognisable as such by his appearance or surroundings.

The Challenge

Now this leads us to a challenge. Look at these 5 seats. Where do you sit?

Are you someone like Herod who is ready to accept that Jesus is real, but feel threatened by the idea of someone else being in control of your life? You've got the power, the possessions, the life you want, everything in place, so you can't bring yourself to put someone else in the power seat?

Are you someone like the people of Jerusalem, content with the lot you've been given? It's not the best, it's not the worst, it's just life! You have accepted the trends and influences of modern culture, you live by the law of the land. Society rules okay. You have maybe heard whispers that there is another authority out there, a different law, a way of living that requires you to readdress your values, and attitudes, and way of life? This rule of Jesus which challenges everything you know, and think, and feel. And this unsettles you.

Perhaps you relate to the religious leaders, fed up with this way of living? Everyday you have this sense that this can't be all there is for you. You want change, you want hope. You're waiting, longing, for things to be better. And you have heard about this Jesus and a new way of living your life, based upon accepting him as King... But, you're not really sure that this is the right thing for you? Perhaps you'll wait a little longer and see if anything else comes along that suits your expectations a bit better?

Maybe you feel akin to the shepherd, who feels unworthy of the grand calling revealed to you. You are someone that the world doesn't seem to appreciate or value. The world doesn't really recognise you, so how important could you possibly be to the God who rules over the entire universe? Thank the Lord that he chose these shepherds, and how wonderful that they received and accepted him. God chose those who didn't have status, or a voice in the community, and he gave them status in the kingdom of heaven and used their voices to proclaim the good news of Christ.

And then the Magi. Maybe their seat seems most comfortable to you? What I like about the Magi is that however it was that they came to find out about Jesus, and whatever preconceptions they had about what he'd be like when they met him, when they did eventually find him they accepted him for who he was. After all their preparation for the long journey they were to travel; the journey itself; the hunting around Jerusalem to locate Jesus; and the realisation that he was not what they were expecting; they accepted him for who he was, worshipped him and offered their gifts. It's astonishing isn't it?

Bible Application

The bible says to the Herods of this world:

> All those who exalt themselves will be humbled, and all those who humble themselves will be exalted[87]

To the People of Jerusalem:

> Those who love their life will lose it, and those who hate their life in this world will keep it for eternal life.[88]

To the religious leaders:

> Jesus said I am the way, the truth and the Life, no-one comes to the Father except through me.[89]

To the shepherds:

> Blessed are the poor in Spirit, for they shall inherit the Kingdom of Heaven, blessed are the meek, for they will inherit the Earth[90]

And, to the Magi:

> *For God so loved the world that he gave his one and only Son Jesus that whoever believes in him shall not perish but have eternal life.[91]*

Conclusion

God did not send Jesus into the world to condemn the world, but to save the world through him. We have the choice in this life to accept King Jesus for who he is, or to reject him. There is no middle ground, but there are eternal consequences for where we choose to sit.

May our Lord Jesus Christ himself and God our Father, who loved us and by His grace gave us eternal encouragement and good hope, encourage your hearts and strengthen you in every good deed and word. May the ministry of the Holy Spirit make you worthy of this calling, and by his power bring to fruition your every desire for goodness and your every deed prompted by faith, to the glory of Jesus name.

JESUS AND THE CHURCH

Luke 2:8-14

And there were shepherds living out in the fields nearby, keeping watch over their flocks at night. An angel of the Lord appeared to them, and the glory of the Lord shone around them, and they were terrified. But the angel said to them, "Do not be afraid. I bring you good news that will cause great joy for all the people. Today in the town of David a Saviour has been born to you; he is the Messiah, the Lord. This will be a sign to you: You will find a baby wrapped in cloths and lying in a manger."

Suddenly a great company of the heavenly host appeared with the angel, praising God and saying,

"Glory to God in the highest heaven, and on earth peace to those on whom his favour rests."

When the angels had left them and gone into heaven, the shepherds said to one another,

"Let's go to Bethlehem and see this thing that has happened, which the Lord has told us about."

So they hurried off and found Mary and Joseph, and the baby, who was lying in the manger. When they had seen him, they spread the word concerning what had been told them about this child, and all who heard it were amazed at what the shepherds said to them.[92]

*****

For many, Christmas marks the end of a busy season. The running around, the preparations, the celebrations... all done. Breath out. Take a load off for a few days before New

Year celebrations. And then, heads down, back to normality.

This is far from being a reflection of the nativity. In Luke 2, the shepherds are visited by a vast heavenly host, declaring the birth of the Messiah. On the year of our Lord, life had carried on much the same as it always had *until* the day of his birth, and *then* all the excitement started. The Messiah had arrived! Christmas was a beginning, not an end! Today we seem to have it all a bit backwards.

Imagine the expectation that the shepherds had for the new year! A sense that *everything* was going to be different. Their expectation was not that the new year would probably be "much the same, though I'm gonna really try to kick that habit, or see that friend more often..." For the shepherds, and those who believed in their message, *all* of life was going to be *radically* transformed, because God had finally sent the long expected Messiah, Jesus.

This is what Christmas is about, and it would be such a shame to miss that because all the presents are opened, the services are over and the sales are on. Christmas is not there to cheer up the end of a year, its there to get our hearts racing and our expectations rising about what God has planned for the next.

Be careful if you are one of those who make resolutions for the new year. So often these resolutions consist of what *we* hope to achieve by *our* will power, for *our* benefit. Two thousand years ago, when Jesus came to the temple, he found a people living by their own values, trying to achieve their own goals in their own ways and for their own glory... and he was not happy with that.

When we look ahead to the new year, if we are going to resolve anything, then may it be to let God do anything *he* wants to do in our lives, by *his* power, and for *his* glory. If you're going to give up anything, give up your rights, give up your own agendas, give up your whole self... give it all up to God.

As we now explore two occasions when Jesus was found amongst the church of his time, lets be challenged by what he expects of his church, and lets get excited and prepared now for the sorts of things that we could be seeing and doing in the new year.

Use the time between Christmas and the New Year to guard yourself against worldly attitudes. Do you really want the new year to be significant? Don't conform to the patterns of this world - eat, drink and be merry throughout Christmas, then change it all with some magical resolutions for the new year - but be transformed by the renewing of your mind. Then you will be able to test and approve what *God's* will is.[93] Pray for that even now, as we explore Jesus and the church.

Challenge 1 – Inward looking.

> *Every year Jesus' parents went to Jerusalem for the festival of the Passover. When he was twelve years old, they went up to the festival, according to the custom. After the festival was over, while his parents were returning home, the boy Jesus stayed behind in Jerusalem, but they were unaware of it. Thinking he was in their company, they travelled on for a day. Then they began looking for him among their relatives and friends. When they did not find him, they went back to Jerusalem to look for him. After three days they found him in the temple courts, sitting among the teachers, listening to them and asking them questions. Everyone who heard him was amazed at his understanding and his answers.[94]*

Parents, who of you have ever been out somewhere and lost your child, even just for a moment? Think back to how you felt. How you responded. On top of the natural sense of anguish, imagine how Mary and Joseph - entrusted with the special responsibility of parenting God's one and only son - would have felt when they realised they had lost him. When Joseph and Mary realised Jesus was not with them, they went back to Jerusalem to look for him.

Imagine the scene. The streets of Jerusalem are jam packed with people who have come for the great passover festival. You've barely managed to claw your way through the bustling crowds and think that your child is with you. The community you live amongst have all travelled together, and now you are all taking yourselves home together... parents leading the way; children running all around you, enjoying each other's company. And then you find your child is not amongst the group. You realise that you haven't in fact seen him all day. Your insides freeze, except for your racing heart. Where is your child? How will you ever find him?

And imagine being the child! 12 years old, and lost amongst the crowds of Jerusalem. You may have even caught sight of your parents ploughing through those bodies towering over you and all around. You begin fighting through the crowds yourself to reach them. You're shouting. Panicking. Desperate to get their attention, before you lose sight of them. And then they're gone, and you're all alone.

But, that's not what we read here of Jesus.

After *three days* of searching, Joseph and Mary found their son in the temple courts sitting amongst the teachers, amazing them with his own teaching. When his parents saw him, they were also astonished. His mother said to him,

> "*Son, why have you treated us like this? Your father and I have been anxiously searching for you.*"[95]

But Jesus is the picture of composure,

> "*Why were you searching for me?*" He asked. "*Didn't you know I had to be in my Father's house?*"[96]

Mary and Joseph are described to be understandably anxious, but Jesus? Settled, calm, being productive, and surprised at his parents for the state *they* are in.

Parents, help your kids to develop their own relationship with their heavenly Father, and to trust in it. Teach them to listen to God, and expect him to speak to them. They are his children first. Teach them to expect his guidance, and be prepared to follow it. Then they will know the true security that comes from God, that overcomes any circumstance.

Encourage any children in your care to know that there are things they can teach you about God. He's too big for any adult to know completely. Children are more innocent in their understanding and less conditioned by the way of this world, so expect that God can use them to teach you more about himself. Children must be brought up to respect and obey their earthly parents, but remember that God is their parent first and foremost. They need to be taught to listen to him, and obey.

And this applies not only to biological parents. In the family of Christ, this applies to younger and older generations too, related or not. Those of you who are older in the faith, do you know you have a responsibility to help nurture the faith of those younger Christians around you? Those newer in their faith, do you know that God can use you to teach those who have been Christians many more years than you? Get to know those around you in your church, and regard each other as those from whom you can learn about God, and how he relates to his people. Above all: everyone, make it your goal to discover God's will for you, for the church, for your community, nation and world. It'll save you a lot of anxiety.

Besides all this, it is important to notice what Jesus had stayed in Jerusalem to do. He was sat in the temple courts with the teachers of the law, and everyone was amazed at what he said. The teachers of the law carried with them the teachings that had been passed down from generation to generation, since the law was first intro-duced. And these teachers were rigid about what they taught. They held the law, and how it was taught it, to be the infallible in-herited truth, and so taught it to the letter.

And yet, here we have Jesus amazing everyone with what *he* taught. It is not that he was working with different material, he was able to reveal an entirely new interpretation of the scrip-tures. He was opening people's eyes to the Spirit of the texts - why they were written, and how they should properly be applied. It is entirely possible for churches to teach the same thing from gener-ation to generation believing that they are faithfully presenting truth, and be utterly amazed should Jesus start speaking amongst that church, and revealing the true heart of the holy scriptures.

What Jesus was teaching and how he went about applying it, was the reason that the religious leaders held him to be a her-etic and blasphemer. Be careful about attuning your ear solely to one manner of teaching, one interpretation of scripture, one application of it. How often has a preacher been poorly received because he presented truths that the congregation were closed to receiving. Valuable God-inspired truths are rejected by the con-gregation because they don't sound like the inherited teachings of that particular church.

I have just qualified us all as teachers of each other in some man-ner. We all have a responsibility before God for what it is we teach others, be it through sermons or informal counsel. All Christians, and especially those on any preaching rota, need to appreciate the huge responsibility they have to teach what is true, regardless of what is inherited.

Every time you reach for your Bible, be it for personal study or preparing an address, make it your earnest prayer for God to guide you in your understanding. Let us not be people who stand as those in the temple courts, completely amazed at the difference between Jesus' teachings and the teaching we hear week in, week out.

> I tell you the truth, that a Christian can't grow,
> If they only accept what they already know.

Challenge two – outward looking.

> *As he taught, Jesus said, "Watch out for the teachers of the law. They like to walk around in flowing robes and be greeted with respect in the market places, and have the most important seats in the synagogues and the place of honour at banquets. They devour widows houses and for a show make lengthy prayers. These men will be punished most severely.*

> *The blind and the lame came to Jesus at the temple, and he healed them.*

Church leaders take note, when the blind and lame came to the temple, they didn't go to the people running it because those people had lost sight of what church was for. Those in need went to Jesus directly, and he healed them. Take people to Jesus. Instil this principle amongst your congregation. The church is here to help direct people to Jesus, knowing that he will gladly meet with them. If, when people come to church, they are not pointed to Jesus, then the church is not doing their job.

If people in church are doing things by their own strength, or doing things because, "well, that's just what we always do at church," you need to challenge that. We all need to be challenged by that. Unless churches are regularly seeing people meeting with Jesus for renewal and restoration, and are regularly seeing the miracles of salvation and all manner of healing, then they should hold very lightly to the way things have always been done.

If you have only been attending church a little while, I urge you to ask people, "What is Jesus like? How can I know him? How can he meet my needs today?" Never mind how warm is the reception, how does the service style suit you, or how good is the coffee... the church is there to help you taste and see that the *Lord* is good! It is a sad day for the church if you are met by a good welcome team when you enter, but leave without ever having met with God.

When this passage talks of the blind and the lame, it is not just those with physical needs that should take note, but those who are spiritually blind and lame. Jesus came for those spiritually blind, who may be physically free to move about but who have never seen what God is like, and feel like they're stumbling through life in the dark. He came for those spiritually lame, who are ever hindered from moving forward, who feel trapped where they are - chained down and unable to break free - perhaps without even knowing exactly why they feel paralysed.

Jesus came to open eyes, and to set people free. And he told his followers to preach the good news and heal the sick. If you find yourself wanting to know him, or you have a need of any kind, pray that Jesus will come and meet you now. And ask a Christian to stand with you in this. It is their commission to do so. And it should be their joy as well.

Every true Christian has the power of the living God in them. It's not about their worldly status, age, or position, it's about the love and power of God, and anyone can ask for him to show that power and love. It doesn't come through lengthy prayers or pomp and show, but in humble submission, and in laying aside our own strengths and weaknesses, appealing to God to reveal himself and apply his power to achieve his will.

Church, know your role. Every Christian must learn to fully accept their position as an heir in God's kingdom. Know the authority you have in Jesus, and the calling you have to live as he did.

Expect more from him this coming year. Help people to come to him. Don't be blind guides. How can you help people come to know God's transformative power, if *you* do not know it or even expect it in your own lives?

God's people are not there merely to look after church buildings, put on a good program of services each week, and protect their own interests within the church walls. God's people are to go outside the walls and make a difference within the community, transforming lives by meeting the needs of the lost and sick, in the name and power of Jesus.

The Shepherd in the field that night had a revelation of the exciting news of Jesus. They didn't stay sat around in the field glorying in what they had experienced, and keeping it amongst themselves. They followed the instruction to go and spread the word; to announce the King and the hope of thorough transformation. Let us, like the shepherds, be excited about the transformation Jesus brings to our own lives, and brings to others through us. Let us proclaim him with due excitement.

Let us pray for the new year, and for his inspiration to fall upon his people, causing us to submit all things to his leading so that we might be transformed. Let us ask him to well up in us an excitement that prompts us to joyfully proclaim the good news amongst the lost. Let us believe in his transformative power, which truly gives people a new life in freedom and nearness to the Messiah, Jesus Christ.

LOCATION, LOCATION, LOCATION

Luke 19:28-38

After Jesus had said this, he went on ahead, going up to Jerusalem. As he approached Bethpage and Bethany at the hill called the Mount of Olives, he sent two of his disciples, saying to them,

"Go to the village ahead of you, and as you enter it, you will find a colt tied there, which no one has ever ridden. Untie it and bring it here, and if anyone asks you, 'Why are you untying it?' say, 'The Lord needs it.'"

Those who were sent ahead went and found it just as he had told them. As they were untying the colt, its owner asked them, "Why are you untying the colt?"

They replied, "The Lord needs it."

They brought it to Jesus, threw their cloaks on the colt and put Jesus on it.
As they went along, people spread their coats on the road. When he came to the place where the road goes down to the Mount of Olives, the whole crowd of disciples began joyfully to praise God in loud voices for all the miracles they had seen:

"Blessed is the king who comes in the name of the Lord!"

"Peace in heaven and glory in the highest."[97]

*****

W hen we think of Palm Sunday, we naturally picture Jesus entering Jerusalem on a donkey whilst the crowds lay their coats down and wave palms in the air to celebrate the arrival of their king.

He was near Jerusalem and the people thought that the kingdom of God was going to appear at once[98]

The crowds believed that their Messiah would immediately establish his reign and overthrow all of their political and military foes. They were anticipating Christ' victory over Israel's localised, physical enemies. But this was not his agenda. I've called this reflection, 'Location, location, location,' because it reviews the whole of the day we celebrate as Palm Sunday, under three headings - the names of three locations significant to the events being described,

> Jericho
> Jerusalem.
> New Jerusalem.

Jericho.

Jesus began the day travelling through Jericho, so this is where we shall begin. The history of Jericho bolsters the expectation of a great military and political champion. Since Israel was conquered and their independence taken, they had been praying for a Messiah. They anticipated a champion like Joshua, Jesus' Old Testament namesake, whom God used to lead his people into the promised land.

The battle of Jericho was Israel's famous victory that began their great conquest to claim the promised land. So, it is with interest to us that Luke 18:35 reveals Jesus' intent to travel through Jericho on his way up to Jerusalem. This is a very symbolic act, and one which lends itself to the anticipation of the Messiah's forceful overthrowing of the powers that held Jerusalem at that time.

We see that the expectation for Jesus to assert his rule in a great display of power is even held amongst his disciples. Jesus had only recently told them that the prophecies about the son of man will be fulfilled:

> *"He will be delivered to the Gentiles. They will mock him, insult him and spit on him; they will flog him and kill him."[99]*

Luke 18:34 states the disciples' failure to receive this information...

> *They did not understand.... Its meaning was hidden.... they did not know what he was talking about.*

By recalling the Old Testament prophecies amongst his disciples, Jesus was providing the proper context of his actions before passing through Jericho, the gateway to his own inheritance.

In reviewing the events following Joshua's conquest of Jericho, we observe some very poignant symbolism, which again helps us understand the type of victory the people expected of Jesus. Having conquered Jericho and Ai, Joshua aroused the fear of the king of Jerusalem, who aligns himself with four other kings to go out and fight the Israelites. The 5 kings were overcome and on the run from Joshua.

> *When Joshua was told that the five kings had been found hiding in the cave at Makkedah, he said, "Roll large rocks up to the mouth of the cave, and post some men there to guard it. But don't stop; pursue your enemies! Attack them from*

the rear and don't let them reach their cities, for the Lord your God has given them into your hand."

So Joshua and the Israelites defeated them completely, but a few survivors managed to reach their fortified cities. The whole army then returned safely to Joshua in the camp at Makkedah, and no one uttered a word against the Israelites.

Joshua said, "Open the mouth of the cave and bring those five kings out to me." So they brought the five kings out of the cave—the kings of Jerusalem, Hebron, Jarmuth, Lachish and Eglon. When they had brought these kings to Joshua, he summoned all the men of Israel and said to the army commanders who had come with him, "Come here and put your feet on the necks of these kings." So they came forward and placed their feet on their necks.

Joshua said to them, "Do not be afraid; do not be discouraged. Be strong and courageous. This is what the Lord will do to all the enemies you are going to fight." Then Joshua put the kings to death and exposed their bodies on five poles, and they were left hanging on the poles until evening.

At sunset Joshua gave the order and they took them down from the poles and threw them into the cave where they had been hiding. At the mouth of the cave they placed large rocks, which are there to this day.[100]

Note the strong imagery here. The authority in Jerusalem was overcome by force. The kings ended up in a cave, the entrance covered with large rocks, and soldiers posted there to guard the cave. God's enemies were made as a foot stool to the commanders of his army. They are dealt with in a brutal yet, to us, familiar manner. Hung on a pole to die, and then put in the cave and concealed again with rocks. Snap back to Jesus' day... Can you imagine what it was like for Jesus' followers to see Jesus, their champion, on the *receiving end* of such a horrific, humiliating and public death? No wonder his followers were so discouraged.

But, what a twist in the tale three days after the crucifixion. Yes, Jesus had been hung on a pole, and placed in the cave. Yet, he did not remain there. The account of the five kings concludes with this,

> they took them down from the poles and threw them into the cave ...At the mouth of the cave they placed large rocks, which are there to this day.

The stones remained as a memorial to God's victory over Old Testament Jerusalem. When people went back to Jesus' cave, there was no such memorial - the rock had been rolled from its place, and he was not to be found.

The City of Palms

That Jericho is revealed in the Old Testament as the City of palms is not incidental to our subject. The significance of palms is vast, then, as we consider Jesus' journeying from the City of Palms, to Jerusalem, where he was received by a crowd waving Palm branches.

> The righteous will flourish like Palm trees.

Palm trees were regarded essential to life in barren places, not least as a means of providing food and shelter. Significantly, they were held to be sacred throughout early history. Palm branches adorned the inner and outer rooms of Solomon's Temple, so the high priest would have to walk between them to enter God's presence. The temple was the place where God dwelt amongst his people, and was that which Jesus famously associated himself when he said,

> *"Destroy this temple, and I will raise it again in three days."[101]*

Palms were, and are still, waved during the feast of tabernacles during which sacrifices are made for sin, and the harvest is gathered - a foreshadowing of the day when palms would be waved for Jesus, the ultimate sacrifice for sin, and bringer of a rich harvest.

Zechariah 14 prophecies that a day will come when the Feast of Tabernacles will be observed by people from all nations, to acknowledge and worship the one true God.

This imagery of palm waving finds its climactic fulfilment in Revelation, the book detailing the establishment of God's eternal kingdom,

> *After this I looked, and there before me was a great multitude that no-one could count, from every nation, tribe, people and language, standing before the throne and before the lamb. They were wearing white robes and were holding palm branches in their hands. And they cried out in a loud voice: "Salvation belongs to our God, who sits on the throne, and to the Lamb."[102]*

Snap back to the road to Jerusalem, where the crowds waved palms and shouted "save us."[103] The call for salvation that echoed the streets of Jerusalem as Jesus rode in, will be conclusively answered on the day he returns. Jesus' entry into Jerusalem pointed not to an immediate victory over Israel's oppressors, but and eternal absolute victory over all evil. He didn't come to claim a temporary throne in Jerusalem, but a throne in the heavenly realm that would never be removed.

Jerusalem.

The symbolism continues. Jerusalem is itself symbolic as God's holy city. Its name comes from *Salem*, meaning peace. 2 Samuel 7:1 speaks of King David's triumphant entry into Jerusalem, which marked the pinnacle of God's victory over Israel's foes,

> *the king was settled in his palace, and the Lord had given him rest from all his enemies around him.*

Again, you can see what was expected of Jesus. David entered Jerusalem half naked and dancing with all his might, saying,

> *"I will celebrate before the lord. I will become even more undignified than this, and I will be humiliated in my own eyes."[104]*

But, contrast that to Jesus entry,

> *as Jesus approached Jerusalem and saw the city, he wept over it.[105]*

One king enters Jerusalem half naked and undignified, carrying the ark of the covenant; the other driven out of the city half naked and undignified, carrying a cross. Again, we associate the two victories, but reveal the new order that Jesus brings.

It is symbolic that Jesus entered Jerusalem upon a colt that had never before been ridden, thus qualifying it for sacred use. His arrival on a donkey, not a horse, was also symbolic. Had Jesus been riding into war, the horse would be the animal of choice. Entering a city on a donkey denoted peace.

Jesus was indeed coming to claim victory that week, but in a new way and over *all* authorities, to bring conclusive peace between

God and man. This is what the people of the day missed. They thought he was coming to rule from Jerusalem, overthrowing the rule of a worldly foe. They limited and localised his victory, according to their current situation. And we can all fall into that trap. How easy to only apply God's victory in light of our own immediate needs, and so similarly localise his dominion and authority according to our desired outcome.

Now, on His way to Jerusalem...[106]

From this point onwards, Jesus' actions and teaching are specifically designed to provide the backdrop for what he was to achieve there. I'm going to briefly take you through the entire order of events as written in Luke's account of the day, beginning from chapter 17, verse 11. As I do so, hold in your mind what we now know to be his intended victory, and the way it was brought into effect. And also, try and be honest about our human condition, and how we often respond to Jesus.

We begin with an immediate display of Jesus' mercy, as he restores ten lepers to health. From the start we must recognise the contrast between compassionate Jesus and the warrior king that is expected. Jesus does establish his great power, but he doesn't use it to overthrow man's power – remember that it is God himself who establishes worldly authorities - he uses it to restore the weak and to transform their lives. We see a glimpse of the victory he intends to secure by exercising his power over the powers of darkness, not merely a worldly foe.

Only one man returns to thank Jesus for his healing. We see that nine out of the ten folk who received a cure from Jesus for their immediate physical needs, went off to enjoy life apart from him. Only one man returned to worship God and follow him. Let us be challenged to not be quick to ask things of God, yet slow to worship him; to receive blessing from God, but not return our full allegiance.

Our greatest needs are not of the body, but the condition of our spirit. And Jesus' ministry of restoration is available to all. These ten men were not only lepers, but Samaritans too. Their condition and their identity both label them outcasts. The man who came to Jesus had been rejected by everyone, and yet Jesus accepted him.

In the following passage, Jesus teaches his followers that the kingdom of God is in their midst; that he is indeed establishing a better kingdom. Yet he also explains that he is soon to suffer and be rejected. They weren't able to grasp this, because this is not how new kingdoms are usually established. They expect the usual pattern of things.

Jesus says he will return, however, and warns them it will be like lightning, and as sudden as the flood of Noah, or the destruction of Sodom by fire - two devastating acts of judgement, by which only the righteous survive. Jesus is broadening the context of his actions across all of history, and reasserting that this is a matter of divine and comprehensive judgement.

Immediately after, in chapter 18, Jesus tells a parable depicting Israel's persistent prayers for the judge to bring justice against her enemies. However, he concludes by asking if the judge will find faith in people when he does appear, or just a people who want their immediate problems with the authorities to be relieved.

Next is the parable of the Pharisee and the tax collector, in which Jesus explains that the religious authority who boasts and trusts in his works and status for salvation will not be accepted, but only the humble sinner who recognises his need for God. Jesus is painting passion week in the light of final judgement, and now is being careful to explain clearly the type of people who will and won't be justified before God.

Jesus' aim is to turn people's expectations on their heads. Those who exalt themselves will be humbled, he says, but those who humble themselves will be exalted. And he will be the ultimate depiction of this when he surrenders himself to a cruel and humiliating death, for the joy set before him. You see how this opposes the view of the religious 'elite,' who believe the messiah is coming to save them on account of their excellence.

Next, Jesus goes on to correct even his disciples, who are preventing people bringing their babies to him for a blessing. He tells them that unless people receive the kingdom of God as babies, (i.e. with simple faith and complete dependence), they won't enter it.

Then, Jesus' encounter with the rich young ruler is described. He has kept all of the commandments since he was young, but Jesus tells him that he won't inherit eternal life for that. He will only be saved by giving away his treasures in order to follow Jesus. Now, Jesus does not discredit the law, or obedience to it, but he turns things around to make it about a person's heart and attitude towards himself, not about mechanical law-keeping or great wealth. Where your heart is, there your treasure lies.

So now, having laid out the context of his second coming, and described the things on which judgement will be based, Jesus focusses in on the days ahead. He reassures his disciples that what will happen to him (the way he'll die, and the purpose of his death) has all been spoken by the prophets throughout the holy scriptures. He's saying, 'don't be alarmed, this is meant to be'. But they don't understand because they too are expecting the culmination of his great miraculous power.

And so Jesus proceeds to Jericho, which he not only symbolically passes through to claim His inheritance, but where he heals a blind beggar. He opens the eyes of a humble yet faith-filled man, symbolising his purpose of bringing sight to the spiritually blind, that they might follow him into his inheritance. It is another picture of who he came for, and how they shall enter the Kingdom.

What is spiritual blindness? It is being blind to who Jesus is. It involves the preoccupation with how the world sees things, failing to see what God is doing and how God does things, because we wear worldly blinkers.

Next, is Jesus' rendezvous with Zacchaeus, who may well have heard about the experience of the rich young ruler, because he gladly gives away his money to follow Jesus. The account provides the contrast of the blind onlookers, who muttered about Jesus associating with sinners.

I think it important to note that Jesus never excluded the financially well off from coming to him but it is evident that, should they hold onto their money as their main treasure, they thus exclude themselves. Jesus said it is harder for a rich man to enter the kingdom of heaven than a for a camel to fit through the eye of a needle. Zacchaeus is an example of the fact that with man it is impossible, but for God all things are possible.

Did you know that it is in this context - the context of Jesus' warnings about his second coming, and about how people do or do not receive him - that Jesus teaches the parable of the 10 minas, or talents as recorded in Matthew 25.

The parable of the ten minas is Jesus' final teaching before he reaches Jerusalem. The challenge of the parable is about how people should live between his resurrection and second coming. I want you to read the parable with this context in mind.

While they were listening to this, he went on to tell them a parable, because he was near Jerusalem and the people thought that the kingdom of God was going to appear at once. He said:

"A man of noble birth went to a distant country to have himself appointed king and then to return. So he called ten of his servants and gave them ten minas. 'Put this money to work,' he said, 'until I come back.'

But his subjects hated him and sent a delegation after him to say, 'We don't want this man to be our king.'
He was made king, however, and returned home. Then he sent for the servants to whom he had given the money, in order to find out what they had gained with it.
The first one came and said, 'Sir, your mina has earned ten more.'

'Well done, my good servant!' his master replied. 'Because you have been trustworthy in a very small matter, take charge of ten cities.'

The second came and said, 'Sir, your mina has earned five more.'

His master answered, 'You take charge of five cities.'

Then another servant came and said, 'Sir, here is your mina; I have kept it laid away in a piece of cloth. I was afraid of you, because you are a hard man. You take out what you did not put in and reap what you did not sow.'

His master replied, 'I will judge you by your own words, you wicked servant! You knew, did you, that I am a hard man, taking out what I did not put in, and reaping what I did not sow? Why then didn't you put my money on deposit, so that when I came back, I could have collected it with interest?'

Then he said to those standing by, 'Take his mina away from him and give it to the one who has ten minas.'

'Sir,' they said, 'he already has ten!'

He replied, 'I tell you that to everyone who has, more will be given, but as for the one who has nothing, even what they have will be taken away. But those enemies of mine who did not want me to be king over them—bring them here and kill them in front of me.'"[107]

This is the king who was being paraded into Jerusalem on palm Sunday.

What does your king look like? If your king does not look like this one then you are in danger of being like the religious leaders who were hostile towards Jesus, or the crowd who didn't understand what type of king he was, or else the apathetic servant who wasted his masters investment. In context, the parable is not merely about being good stewards of what you are given, but living in anticipation of coming judgement. You might consider this a grim message about Palm Sunday. Surely not.

Often when judgement is touched upon, people get caught up on the doom and gloom of it. Please recognise that Judgement is only doom and gloom if you choose to live outside of Jesus' Lordship. Jesus' teaching is a warning, but it is one by which he says, 'take and use what I have to offer, and you will be rewarded.' It is as much an encouragement as a warning, and how you receive it might reflect an inner conviction about whom from the parable you most relate to.

If you accept Jesus as the king that he is, then judgement for you is a joyful welcome. You shall enter the great wedding feast, and an eternity in God's kingdom. But, those of you who have not yet received him as such, do not wait to receive him for truly he will come suddenly at a time unknown to us. How long will you risk waiting, considering what awaits those who fail to receive the king?

The New Jerusalem

> *Don't be conformed to the pattern of this world, but be transformed by the renewing of your mind.[108]*

Stop expecting things to be done by the usual worldly patterns.

See how God does things, and what he is doing it for! Do not trivialise Christ's victory. Jesus' actions secured absolute eternal victory and established his Lordship over all of creation and the principalities and powers of this world; both the heavens and the earth are subject to his rule, and always will be.

There are attitudes in those waving palms for Jesus, which resonate with us when we fail to consider the totality of Christ' victory. We can, like them, all too easily focus on our need to be rescued from our immediate conflict, and overlook the full eternal scale of Christ's victory.

We can focus so intently on the here and now, that we loose sight of the heavenly order. We need to stop looking at heaven through the lens of what's happening on earth, and start looking at earth through the lens of what's happening in heaven. We must stop trying to bring the heavenly into the context of earth, and start bringing the earthly into the context of heaven. Do you see the difference?

Both Jesus' and Joshua's victory happened at passover, a festival celebrating God's deliverance of Israel from their oppressors by the sacrificial blood of a lamb! Indeed, the correlation between the physical events of Palm Sunday with God's eternal plan, from beginning to end, cannot be overstated. So with every moment, we must consider our immediate situation in light of this eternal plan that God is revealing throughout our world's history.

As Christians in an individualistic era, we can be so caught up on our own personal redemption through Christ, that we belittle his universal victory over all powers of this world. We pray for our own sanctification, yet might be thrown into panic by the idea of praying with someone for their healing, or deliverance from spiritual forces. Even the idea that there is a spirit world, in which war is raging over us, is something we can often completely neglect, yet should be our focus. Christ's victory was the means by which he empowered us to live as he did whilst we are on earth.

Our panic or uncertainty comes from our inward looking idea of status before God. We might find ourselves asking,

- Can I actually pray for this?
- Am I in the right place before God?
- Do Christians even do this stuff any more?

Your personal holiness is indeed of importance, and we should diligently seek to be holy as he is holy. But if you come to pray for healing based on *your* credentials, you've lost before you've started. Yes, you can pray for healing today or deliverance from powers of darkness, because of *Christ's* universal victory over sin and death. Make it about *him* and the authority you have in *him*, not about how you feel you measure up according to your works.

Making your Christianity primarily about you, not only robs you of the authority given you by Christ, but is the catalyst for all sorts of tensions within the church body. How devastating when our individual opinions and preferences lead us into conflict or separation from those who approach Jesus' cross and throne from a different direction.

Receive Christ to help you overcome that foe which is personal to you. Come to Christ as you are. Delight that he has made you a unique individual. But understand that his victory is meant to unite those who trust in him. It is his command that we be united as diverse parts of his own body. Regard no-one from a worldly point of view.

> *Though once we regarded Christ in this way, we do so no longer. Therefore, if anyone is in Christ, the new creation has come. The old has gone, the new is here! All this is from God who reconciled us to himself through Christ and gave us the ministry of reconciliation.*
>
> *We are therefore Christ's ambassadors, as though God was making his appeal through us. As God's co-workers we urge*

you not to receive God's grace in vain, for he says,

"In the time of my favour, I heard you, and in the day of salvation, I helped you."

I tell you, now is the time of God's favour, now is the day of salvation.[109]

Jesus came as a humble but decisive victor, conquering the forces of darkness through sacrifice and submission to the Father. He rode into Jerusalem to transform the way people viewed their lives and situations - from their localised, earthly perspective to a universal, heavenly perspective. He called the lost to him, called his church to unity in him, and empowered it with his own authority to continue in his example. Is this the king you welcome? Is this the life you are prepared to live? This is the day of God's favour. Let us accept and live in it.

JESUS RAISES LAZARUS

John 11:1-44

Now a man named Lazarus was sick. He was from Bethany, the village of Mary and her sister Martha. (This Mary, whose brother Lazarus now lay sick, was the same one who poured perfume on the Lord and wiped His feet with her hair.) So the sisters sent word to Jesus, "Lord the one you love is sick."

When he heard this, Jesus said, "This sickness will not end in death. No, it is for God's glory so that God's son may be glorified through it."[110]

*****

In this story we see that Jesus knew a bad thing had happened to someone he cared about, and he knew that other people were distressed because of it. So Jesus went to be with those people, to cry with them, and yet reassure them that all would be okay. He was able to do this because he knew God was with them, and he knew what was going on and the reason for it. Jesus was confident that God wants only what is best for us, and is powerful to help us, so we can thank and Praise him even in our most bitter circumstance.

Contrary to worldly understanding, the Bible teaches that we can have joy when bad things happen, because God works even bad things for good to make us stronger and braver than if they had never happened. Have you ever been temped to ask, "Where was God when that bad thing happened?" I have.

"Oh God, why did you allow this?"
"If you're good, how could you put me through this?"

Despite what we learn about God - about his love, and goodness, and power and wisdom- there's still this very real part of us that likes to say, "God, if you had been there, this wouldn't have happened." This was certainly true of Martha and Mary. They both said to Jesus,

"If you had been here, my brother would not have died."

The first thing I want to say is a word of encouragement, don't let the devil tell you that if you say this type of thing to God, then you are an unfaithful person and should carry a great burden of guilt. Martha and Mary say this to Jesus *because* they believed that he is the Son of God, and powerful to act. Their statement does not show a lack of faith in Jesus, rather proof of their recognition that he did indeed have power to heal their brother. They had not turned their back on Jesus, rather they are bringing the situation to him that he may reveal his purposes through it. Their statement does not cut him out, but welcomes him in!

Be encouraged, if you are ever angry or confused at what God is doing, on some level you prove yourself as a person who believes he is loving and just, and powerful enough to turn your situation to good. Just don't remain in your anger. You will need to accept that he does things a little differently to us. So, lets now consider the text and look at what it says about Jesus, and what he was in fact doing. I'll highlight three attributes of Jesus revealed by the story,

1. Jesus knows.
2. Jesus cares.
3. Jesus acts.

He knows you and what you're going through; he cares about you and your life; and he acts on your behalf and for your best interests.

So firstly, Jesus knows.

Earlier in the chapter Jesus said,

> *"This sickness will not end in death. No, it is for God's glory, so that the Son of Man may be glorified through it."[11:1]*

Jesus knows the end of the story before it happens, and his agenda throughout is God's glory. This is an important concept that we need to hold on to as events unfold. He has a greater perspective, and so does not act in the way that was expected of him by those who are worldly minded.

Jesus brings the reassurance that Lazarus' sickness would not end in death. We can understand, then, if people breathed a sigh of relief, thinking that Lazarus would get better. And perhaps we can relate to how people must have felt when Lazarus died! Have you ever said to God,

> *"But you said....!????"*

Well, lets look at what Jesus did say! Notice that he didn't say, "Lazarus will not die." He said that the sickness would not *end* in death. The challenge here is to hold Jesus to his word *until he fulfils it*, not until we reach a point along the way where the evidence seems to suggest we heard wrong.

How often have you thought God is going to act in a certain way, and gotten a surprise when he doesn't? I have often asked God to act in a certain way and later thanked him that, because of his grace, he didn't. Jesus knows every detail of the situation, and knows from the start how he should act, how it will end, and why it was occurring. The same is true today.

Remember the story of Jesus healing the soldier's servant without ever needing to be there with him. Jesus does not need to go to

Lazarus to heal him. Furthermore, he waits until he knew that Lazarus had died *before* he began the journey to see him. So why does he go at all? He goes because he knows how it will end.

Jesus knows how Martha and Mary would naturally respond to their brother's death, and so goes to be with them. He draws near to them in their suffering because he knows how they are feeling, and *then* he deals with Lazarus. Be assured that Jesus knows the pain you feel while you wait for the fulfilment of his promises, and how you feel when it seems they have failed. Your pain doesn't motivate him to fulfil the promise quicker, but to draw close to you while you wait.

When Martha comes out to meet Jesus, he says to her,

"Your brother will rise again."[112]

Earlier, the passage reveals that Lazarus is a man that Jesus loves; he is someone personally dear to Jesus. But here Jesus refers to Lazarus as Martha's brother. He acknowledges her connection with Lazarus and the personal nature of the situation. Jesus does not merely respond to situations according to how he feels about them, but also with a deep awareness of how they personally effect everyone else involved.

Jesus says, "Your brother will rise again," and this inspires Martha to think outside of her immediate perspective. She says,

"I know he will rise again, in the resurrection at the last day!"[113]

She has come to regard the situation through an eternal perspective, and thus Jesus has created the opportunity to reveal more eternal truths about himself. He says,

"I am the resurrection and the life. The one who believes in me will live, even though they die; and whoever lives by believing in me will never die."[114]

Communicating this message is Jesus' agenda throughout these events, and indeed throughout every event in all our lives. His eternal agenda is that we may come to know that he is the Son of God and that if we believe in him we will live with him throughout eternity, even though these earthly bodies will die. Everything Jesus does is to save you from an eternal death, and to implore you to take hold of an eternal life with him. Why? Because of point 2,

Jesus cares.

As soon as Jesus reveals to Martha who he is, he asks,

"Do you believe this?"[115]

Remember that Jesus had said that Lazarus' illness would not end in death and, at this point, Lazarus is indeed dead. What a time to ask if Martha believes in what he says to her! And what a faithful response she gives. Martha says,

"yes, Lord"[116]

And she goes away. Jesus has not clarified that he is about to raise her brother from the dead, but because of his careful actions and words Martha has gone away satisfied that whatever is happening, Jesus can be fully trusted as the Messiah. She has faith that, even if things do not pan out the way she had hoped, and Jesus had not acted the way she initially wanted him to, she could still find peace in the knowledge that he is the Son of God, trustworthy in all he does. This is a much more solid peace than that which is swayed by the outcome of every circumstance we face. It proves Jesus' care and it helps us to understand why he said,

> *"Lazarus is dead, and for your sake I am glad that I was not there, so that you may believe."[117]*

He asks Martha, "Do you believe in me, and what I'm saying?" And he asks us the same questions today.

Now, Martha chose to come out to Jesus, but Mary has stayed in her home and in her grief, and in the company of those who are grieving with her. Have you ever acknowledged that Jesus is wanting to draw near, and chosen to stay in your place of sorrow? But Jesus still cares. He hasn't written her off, but asks her to come to him. And what's her response? She quickly gets up and goes. She had not gone out to him by her own initiative like Martha, but when his invite comes, she doesn't allow her sorrow to overrule it. She gets up quickly from the place and the people and the emotions that she has surrounded herself with, and hastens to Jesus.

She too tells Jesus that if he had been there, her brother would not have died. And speaking the words aloud brings her back to tears. Jesus sees her. She is not alone in her pain. She is not invisible to God. Jesus sees her, and he is deeply moved. Do you know that Jesus is deeply moved when he sees you upset? He is moved because he loves you, and because he was once a man on this earth who experienced what you and I go through. He empathises with us. He rejoices with us, and he cries with us. He cares.

> *Jesus wept.[118]*

The Jews in the crowd acknowledge that Jesus is weeping because he loved Lazarus. Jesus weeps because of the effects that this fallen world has on the people whom he loves. That's all of us. It is not a weeping borne out of desperation because we are doomed to remain prisoners to the effects of sin, but it is a choice he makes to emotionally engage with his beloved creation, whom he designed and made to have perfect unity with himself.

Jesus is then,

> *once more deeply moved.[119]*

Do you know that Jesus is deeply moved when he sees you upset? Not just once as a sentimental gesture before he knuckles down and starts helping, No! Rather he remains deeply moved throughout the whole duration of our pain, whilst he is acting on our behalves. It may be a most valuable exercise to try and consider how much more deeply Jesus feels about things than we do.

Jesus goes to the tomb and says,

> *"Take away the stone."[120]*

But Martha says,

> "Lord, by this time there is a bad odour."[121]

She gives him good reason to keep his distance, because she loves him too, but Jesus perseveres anyway. Do you know that Jesus is prepared to go above and beyond for you? Way above and beyond, no matter what? Look at the cross.

> *"Did I not tell you that if you believe, you will see the glory of God?"[122]*

He reminds them of what he had said, so to bring what he's about to do into its proper context. When Jesus was told that Lazarus was sick, he recognised that if he was to go immediately and heal him, there was a danger of people following him only because he could satisfy their immediate needs. When Jesus fed the 5,000, he said to people not to follow him because they had their fill, but to follow him because they believed in the one that God had sent.

Jesus loves you too much to immediately remove all suffering from you, because he knows that it is in your best interest to develop in you an attitude that, whatever you are going through, you will trust in God. He wants to grow in you the understanding that he is just, and that your reliance on him and your reward for it, is much better for you than having a cosy life.

> "Did I not tell you that if you believe, you will see the glory of God?"[123]

So Jesus now sets the example for us in prayer.

> "Father, I thank You"[124]

Are these your first words during a time of weeping? Father, thank you! He says,

> "You have heard me. I knew that you always hear me...."[125]

Be assured, he *always* hears you.

> "... but I said this for the benefit of the people standing here, that they may believe that you sent me."[126]

See how meticulously Jesus is establishing the reasons for all that he has done, before he performs the miraculous. Be encouraged, everything you are going through, and all of God's actions throughout, are to bring you to a place of total belief in him, perhaps not for your immediate satisfaction, but certainly for your eternal satisfaction.

Can we just recognise the overwhelming fact that God has determined that, in every second of our lives, he will only ever act for the good of us that love him! Because Jesus lives forever, he has a permanent priesthood. Therefore, Jesus is able to save completely those who come to God through him, because he always lives to intercede for them.

And so to our third point, Jesus acts

Jesus raises Lazarus.

> *"Lazarus, come out!"[127]*

And he does!

Bearing in mind what we have already looked at, never interpret God's 'failure' to intervene the way you would wish, as proof that he does not have power to act. "Lazarus, come out!" It is easy to picture Lazarus lying in the tomb, and easy to picture him walking out of the tomb with some bandages hanging from him, like some scene from a movie. But do we actually give much thought to the bit in-between?

Lazarus was dead! He has been dead for four days! He's decaying, and starting to smell! When Jesus tells Lazarus to come out, in the words of the Bible,

> *the dead man came out.[128]*

Do you know that Jesus is so powerful that even the dead hear his voice, and do what he says! The rotting flesh of Lazarus' body with no life in it, undergoes a complete restoration. The skin and flesh heal, the heart starts to beat again, the brain awakens, the mouth breathes air once more into revived lungs. The mind, soul, and spirit are restored. Do you see the power of Jesus!?

One commentator observed that had Jesus not specified "*Lazarus*, come out", then anyone else laid dead in that tomb at the time would have come out with him! The dead hear Jesus voice and act on what he says. Do the dead perhaps know something we don't?

The bible describes us all as the dead until salvation. Though breath be in our lungs, and blood pumps around our body, we are dead in our sins if we have not listened to Jesus' voice and received his words of life. If that is you then let it be said, you are spiritually dead! And this death is eternal. But those who accept the invitation to come to Jesus, believing in him as God's son and accepting him as Messiah, will very really be amongst those who were once called dead and are now made alive by His power.

Jesus says to the crowd,

> "*Take off the grave clothes and let him go.*"[129]

And I don't think Jesus was solely referring to the grave clothes Lazarus is wearing. I think the crowd are wearing grave clothes too! You see, before we come to Christ and believe in him as our saviour, we are dead in our transgressions and sin, prone to always act in disbelief according to our sinful natures; to reject God and prefer our own way of life. We are completely wrapped in grave clothes of doubt, fear, selfish motives, shame, pride etc. But to you who have been made alive in Christ, "Take off the grave clothes". Live no longer bound in disbelief, doubt and weakness, swayed by every circumstance, but stand as one who is alive, strong in your belief in God, and determined to live for his glory in every situation.

So we conclude with a question.

Are *you* still wearing any grave clothes? Do you still hold on to the rags this world has dressed you in, which keep you from living a full and holy life by Jesus' power? Perhaps you don't yet know Christ as your saviour and are still in the tomb! Don't remain there any longer, still wrapped in grave clothes. Ask God, and he will respond to your every need, for the sake of your eternal life and the sake of his glory. Jesus knows, Jesus cares, and Jesus acts. Whether right this instant you are Christian or not, will you believe in him?

GAINING GROUND, ONE FOOT AT A TIME

John 13:1-5

It was just before the passover Festival. Jesus knew that the hour had come for him to leave this world and go to the Father. Having loved his own who were in the world, he loved them to the end.

The evening meal was in progress, and the devil had already tempted Judas, the son of Simon Iscariot, to betray Jesus. Jesus knew that the Father had put all things under his power, and that he had come from God and was returning to God; so he got up from the meal, took off his outer clothing, and wrapped a towel around his waist. After that, he poured water into a basin and began to wash his disciples' feet, drying them with the towel that was wrapped around him.[130]

*****

Who is this Jesus?
What did he come to do?
And what is our response?

Those are the questions by which we come to this passage. They were the questions people were asking back in first century Palestine. They were extremely hot questions during this particular time of passover with massive implications, as indeed they have today. The setting of this passage in John is extremely useful in helping us to explore the answers.

Well, we start with **Who is Jesus?** What does this passage teach us about him?

The first thing we learn from the passage is that the Passover festival is looming. Well, let's unpack the scene a little. It is a time when many Jewish people have come to Jerusalem for a festival in order to remember and celebrate when God intervened to save his people, Israel. In a display of incredible power God performed great miracles through his servant Moses, to give his people freedom from the rule of their enemies, the Egyptians. Jews from all over have now come to pray for deliverance from their own oppressors, the Romans.

Passages such as Isaiah 63:7-15, in which the Israelites cry out to the Lord for deliverance, capture that sense of, 'When, Oh God, will you come and save us the way you saved our ancestors from Egypt?'

Look down from heaven and see, from your lofty throne, holy and glorious.
Where are your zeal and your might? Your tenderness and compassion...?[131]

The Jews are asking the same of God now; that God would come and release them from the rule of Rome. And yet, there is Jesus right there with them - God amongst them, come to save - but they didn't see it.

In Exodus 7 we see God beginning to prepare Moses for his intervention against the Egyptians before the first passover. The Lord said to Moses,

"See, I have made you like God to Pharaoh... But I will harden Pharaoh's heart and though I multiply my signs and wonders, he will not listen to you..... and I will bring out my divisions, my people the Israelites."[132]

In first century Palestine, it is the Jew's hearts that were hardened even though, through Jesus, God was showing himself through signs and wonders. Their own eyes were closed.

> *Where are your zeal and your might?*
> *Your tenderness and compassion...?*

Though they ask two questions of God, it is clear that their hopes had been placed only in the answer to one. They awaited a zealous and mighty Messiah, yet failed to recognise him *because* he displayed tenderness and compassion. Jesus did not exert his zeal and might in the manner they expected from their warrior King, so for all his tenderness and compassion, they rejected his claim of being the Messiah as blasphemy.

In Isaiah 43 God said,

> *"Forget the former things.... See, I am doing a new thing, do you not perceive it?... Review the past and state your case.... I disgraced the dignitaries of your temple, Jacob to destruction and Israel to scorn."[133]*

The Jews are looking back, and they do not perceive that God is doing a new thing through Jesus. The zeal and might, tenderness and compassion cried out for in Isaiah, are all perfectly expressed in Jesus Christ. It is a misunderstanding of these contrasting yet complimentary attributes that tripped up the Jews, and also the disciples. Indeed it easily trips us up as well.

Throughout the gospels we see that, for the Jews, it wasn't Jesus' power that tripped them up, it was his claims that he was God.

> *Again his Jewish opponents picked up stones to stone him, but Jesus said to them,*

> *"I have shown you many good works from the Father. For which of these do you stone me?"*

> *"We are not stoning you for any good work," they replied, "but for blasphemy, because you, a mere man, claim to be God."[134]*

In Matthew 16, we see that, for Peter, the reverse was true - it wasn't Jesus' claims that he was God which tripped him up, but his power:

> *"But what about you?" [Jesus] asked. "Who do you say I am?"*
>
> *Simon Peter answered, "You are the Messiah, the Son of the living God."*
>
> *....*
>
> *From that time on Jesus began to explain to his disciples that he must go to Jerusalem and suffer many things at the hands of the elders, the chief priests and the teachers of the law, and that he must be killed and on the third day be raised to life.*
>
> *Peter took him aside and began to rebuke him. "Never, Lord!" he said. "This shall never happen to you!"[135]*

The Jews thought Jesus too powerless to lead and conquer, the disciples thought he was too powerful to serve and suffer. Neither the Jews nor disciples thought that it was right for their King to be a humble servant.

It is very difficult, but very important, to hold the two together. Jesus is not somewhere in the middle of a mighty/meek scale, he is both extremes held in perfect unison. John Chapters 12 and 13 are remarkably good at showing how the two dynamics of power and tenderness are expressed in the person and ministry of Jesus; how he could indeed be both; how a king can indeed be a servant.

A tale of two sittings!

In John Chapters 12 and 13, two accounts of two meals stand side by side. The two passages mirror each other, yet highlight the seemingly opposing characteristics of Jesus. One meal projects

Jesus as a King to be honoured, and one meal projects him as a servant of his people. There are striking comparisons to be made between the two accounts, which start to unpack this a little.

Chapter 12
The King to be honoured

Chapter 13
The King who is a servant

Verse 1
Six days before passover

Verse 1
Just before the Passover feast

Verse 3
Mary took about a pint of pure nard, an expensive perfume; she poured it on Jesus' feet and wiped his feet with her hair.

Verse 5
[Jesus] poured water into a basin and began to wash the disciples' feet and dry them with the towel that was around him

Verse 4
(Not seeing the significance...) one of his disciples, Judas Iscariot, who was later to betray him, objected.

Verse 8
(not seeing the significance, one of his disciples objected)
"Never shall you wash my feet!" Peter told him

Verse 23
"The hour has come for the Son of Man to be glorified"

Verse 31
"Now the Son of Man is glorified"

Chapter 12 speaks of Jesus as the king of power, who raised one of the other guests, Lazarus, from the dead. A meal was given in his honour, and he was being served. A very expensive perfume was brought out and poured on his feet by a woman, who proceeded to humble herself before him and wipe his feet with her hair. Here is a noble King. How fitting that a few verses later we read of a crowd welcoming him into Israel, shouting:

"Hosannah"

"Blessed is he who comes in the name of the Lord!"

"Blessed is the King of Israel"[136]

Yet, even during this meal we see great examples of his tenderness and compassion. John 11:3 described Lazarus as 'the one Jesus loves' and whom he wept over alongside Lazarus' family when he died. At this same meal, Jesus defends Mary when Judas rebukes her for 'wasting' her valuable perfume.

Not only does Jesus prove and exert his authority, he does so to protect his servant. Here is not a King whose power separates him from his subjects, but one who stands beside them. He is powerful yet kind; passionate yet Loving. One may say, zealous; mighty; tender; compassionate.

Chapter 12 begins with Jesus' honour, and also reveals his compassion. In contrast, Chapter 13 first reflects upon Jesus' love and gives account of his extraordinary servant-heartedness, yet also states the extent of his power.

Having loved his own who were in the world, he loved them to the end[137]

He poured water into a basin and began to wash his disciples' feet. [138]

Jesus knew that the Father had put all things under his power.[139]

Just imagine, as we sit here right now, that you knew God had put all things under your power. *All things* under *your* power. What do you do with that? What is the first thing you do with power over all things?

Well, let us now look at: **What did Jesus come to do?**

Jesus came to change the entire world and put *everything* right. And he succeeded. Look, you can read it here in John 13,

> *Jesus knew that the Father had put all things under his power; so he got up from the meal, took off his outer clothing (He's getting serious) wrapped a towel around his waist (Wait, what?), poured water into a basin (huh??), and began to wash and dry his disciples' feet (say again????).*

Um, in the ministry of bringing the whole world back into order and undoing the power of darkness, that's not exactly what my first move would have been. Well, thank goodness it was him and not me at that dinner table. You see, Jesus *was* changing the whole world. He was gaining ground one foot at a time! How does washing his disciples feet change the world? He says, in verses 13-16,

> *"You call Me Teacher and Lord, and rightly so, because I am. So if I, your Lord and teacher, have washed your feet, you also should wash one another's feet. I have set you an example so that you should do as I have done for you."*

And there is a promise.

> *"If you know these things, you will be blessed if you do them."[140]*

In Matt 23:12 Jesus says,

> *"For those who exalt themselves will be humbled, and those who humble themselves will be exalted."*

Jesus is changing the world here. He's changing the paradigm of where real power and blessing lies. Jesus was the greatest, and yet he made himself the least. He is teaching a message of submission to one another. He is giving application for the beatitudes. It is not a call for us to just symbolically wash our friends feet, it is a call for us to completely put ourselves below one another.

The apostle Paul continues this teaching,

> *In humility value others above yourselves not looking to your own interests but each of you to the interests of the others. In your relationships with one another, have the same mindset as Christ Jesus[141]*

Hear these words about Jesus:

> *He was with God in the beginning. Through him all things were made. In him was life. The Son is the radiance of God's glory. But since the children have flesh and blood, he too shared their humanity. A baby wrapped in cloths. Being in very nature God, he did not consider equality with God something to be used to his own advantage; rather, he made himself nothing by taking the very nature of a servant, being made in human likeness. And being found in appearance as a man, he humbled himself by becoming obedient to death, even death on a cross! God presented Christ as a sacrifice of atonement through the shedding of his blood. He was put to death in the body but made alive in the spirit. IT*

> *IS FINISHED. And God exalted him to the highest place and gave him the name which is above every name, the son of man, dressed in a robe reaching down to his feet and with a golden sash around his chest. The hair on his head was white like wool, as white as snow, and his eyes were like blazing fire. His feet were like bronze glowing in a furnace, and his voice was like the sound of rushing waters. In his right hand he held seven stars, and coming out of his mouth was a sharp, double edged sword. His face was like the sun, shining in all its brilliance. At the name of Jesus every knee should bow, in heaven and on earth and under the earth, and every tongue acknowledge that Jesus Christ is Lord, to the glory of God the Father.[142]*

In view of this, let's consider again Jesus' actions at the last supper. Jesus knew that the Father had put all things under his power, and that he had come from God and was returning to God, so he got up, took off his outer clothing, wrapped a towel around his waist, and began to wash his disciples feet. When he had finished, he put on his clothes and returned to his place.

'Oh God, Where is your Zeal and might, your tenderness and compassion?'

In a small room, washing dirt off of peoples feet.

What is our response?

Jesus finished the work of his incarnate ministry, and he is exalted in heaven. The washing of the disciples feet was a picture of Jesus' whole ministry. It was an example to us.

> *The son of man did not come to be served, but to serve. You my brothers and sisters were called to be free. But do not use your freedom to indulge the flesh; rather serve one another*

humbly in love. Each of you should use whatever gifts you have received to serve others. Elders, shepherd God's flock, eager to serve, being examples to the flock. Those who have served well gain an excellent standing and great assurance in their faith in Jesus Christ. Be devoted to one another in love. Honour one another above yourselves. Never be lacking in ZEAL, but keep your spiritual fervour, serving the Lord.[143]

If you are anything like me, there's a little something nagging at you inside. A little something that says,

"I know that I am to serve and prefer everyone over myself, but, you see, its very difficult!"

The problem goes right back to Adam and Eve. God made mankind in his own image, but they disobeyed him. He said "Don't eat the fruit." They ate the fruit. In doing so, they despised the image of God and, recognising themselves to be naked, sewed fig leaves together to cover their shame. They traded the image of God for fig leaves! And like Adam and Eve, we too are fallen. We have within us a sinful, selfish nature that sees something sweet and wants it; that thinks we know what is best for ourselves and tries to take it; that hears the word of God, and ignores it so we can get what we want.

We have our own fig leaves. Things of this world that are designed to cover our shame. We grasp at power, at wealth, at possessions, at self adulation, at the praise of others. And we sew it all together into a garment that we think makes us look pretty good. But they are just fig leaves, and are there to protect our pride and cover our shame. The way we obtain them is usually by putting ourselves before others and preferring our own needs over theirs.

Jesus' example and command to us is to take off these garments, and serve one another. We can only lay down dirty garments of selfishness, and yet the amazing promise is that if we are prepared to lay them down, they are thrown away and exchanged for new robes of righteousness.

> I delight greatly in the Lord, my soul rejoices in my God, for He has clothed me with garments of salvation, and arrayed me in a robe of righteousness.[144]

Those of you who are aware of their inability to lay down what you have clothed yourself in, and serve one another wholeheartedly... be encouraged. Help is at hand. When Jesus appeared to the disciples after his resurrection, he said to them,

> "I am going to send to you what my Father has promised; but stay in the city until you have been clothed with power from on high."[145]

God has sent to us the Holy Spirit, to empower us to do what he asks of us, and to follow Jesus' example. If you have not received the Holy Spirit of power, how will you follow the example of the Holy Son of God. No, you must receive his power.

> "As the Father sent me, I am sending you." And with that he breathed on them and said, "Receive the Holy Spirit. If you forgive anyone's sins, their sins are forgiven: if you do not forgive them, they are not forgiven."[146]

Are you shocked by that? This a significant warning to you and I, who desire to be recipients of God's power. Will you be impacted by the enormous implications of how we behave toward one another. Jesus did not say,

> 'follow my example if you can, as best as you can, because then everyone will be much happier. But if you can't, well, don't worry I'll tidy up the rough edges. No real harm done.'

No! He said,

> "I have set you an example that you should do as I have done for you. No servant is greater than his master."[147]

If the master did these things, how much more should his servants do them. You must do this. It is important. And this issue of forgiveness helps to illustrate the point. What is Jesus saying when he says they won't be forgiven unless you forgive them? Is it that if I do not forgive my brothers and sisters, they will not be forgiven by God? I think John chapter 13 points towards the answer. When Peter resists Jesus' attempts at washing his feet, Jesus says,

> "unless I wash you, you have no part with me."[148]

Peter replies,

> "Then Lord, wash my hands and my head as well!"[149]

But Jesus says,

> "Those who have had a bath need only to wash their feet; their whole body is clean. And you are clean."[150]

Now in those days, dirty feet would have been a constant issue. people walking round in sandals, along dirty roads, pathways, fields, and the like, would have picked up a lot of dirt on their feet. They may have had a bath that morning and their whole body be clean, but by lunchtime their feet are black. They wouldn't need another bath to make themselves clean, but would only need a foot wash.

Now, what Jesus is saying to Peter is that he is clean. He has accepted Jesus as Lord and so is made righteous. He has received salvation, and so the whole of him is clean. Peter's problem and ours is that, in walking the paths of our lives here on earth, we tend to pick up dirt along the way - marks of the world that make us unclean. We still hold Jesus to be our saviour, but we are constantly putting our foot in it, if you like. We sin. We drag our feet in the mud and get them dirty.

Now, we do not need to receive salvation all over again - to have our whole sinful nature dealt with and cleansed. No, that's been done. But we do need to be sanctified, and have those marks of our sinful acts washed away. We need to have our feet cleaned, but only our feet cleaned, and our whole bodies are clean again.

If Jesus washing the disciples' feet is a picture of sanctification, can we really do like Jesus? Can we really have a part in the sanctification of our brothers and sisters, and wash one another's feet? Well, Jesus tells us to. He tells us that unless we forgive people, they will not be forgiven! If we do not forgive our brothers and sisters, we do not rob them of their salvation, but we do perhaps leave dirt on their feet, and on our own too.

Think about a situation where you know you have wronged someone and you have asked their forgiveness, but they have refused to give it you. Now, before God you are still saved, but the knowledge of someone holding something against you can easily become a mark on you that sticks, and weighs you down. Do not take lightly the importance of your behaviour towards others; your responsibility to wash their feet, and prefer their needs, and act in love towards them. Never allow Satan to lead you into a situation where you feel justified for 'having dirt on someone,' let alone spreading it. This is blatant disobedience. Woe to the one who continues in their unforgiveness and dares to pray,

> *"Forgive us our trespasses, as we forgive those who trespass against us."*

In writing this, I am impacted and convicted strongly of my responsibility in this. I know my need to persist in praying for the

Holy Spirit to fill me anew with Christ's power, so that I can forgive others whom I have held things against, and safely pray for the same forgiveness from God. I must ask for the daily assurance that this task is not beyond me. I must ask that by God's own power, I will be able to stand before God one day knowing I have fought the good fight, I have finished the race, and kept the faith; That there is in store for me a crown of righteousness, given to me through Christ; That God would say of me, "Well done, good and faithful servant." I urge you to join me in making this a prayer priority.

Perhaps you are someone who cannot say that they have ever been washed in this way, by receiving Christ as your saviour and the justification he gives. Maybe this day you have become aware of the dirt in your life for the first time, and want to be rid of it before it builds up. Maybe you have been aware of it for a while, and it is weighing your feet down, weighing your whole body down, and making it a real struggle to walk through life. I urge you, bring it to God now. Don't persist in carrying that burden. Take the opportunity to be free of it through the power and ministry of Jesus, the only way by which we can be saved.

Wherever you may be reading this, and whatever the state of your life, God will hear your prayer and be swift in receiving you, washing you clean of your sin, and committing himself wholly to you as his redeemed, adopted child. Simply reach out to him I prayer...

> *Dear Father God, I accept that you are real, and wanting a relationship with me. I also accept that you are holy, and my dirt, my sin, has caused a separation between us. I thank you for sending your son, Jesus, that he would die in place of sinners, paying the penalty for those who trust in him as their saviour, and raising them with him to eternal life. I put my trust in him now, so please forgive me, and accept me into your family. I accept the Holy Spirit as a seal of my*

salvation, and ask for him to empower me to live as Christ Jesus lived. Thank you for receiving me, Father, as your child. Amen.

TEARS TO JOY, PART ONE
John 16:16-24

*[Jesus said to His disciples] "A little while, and you will no longer see me; and again a little while, and you will see me."
Some of His disciples then said to one another, "What is this thing he is telling us, 'A little while, and you will not see me; and again a little while, and you will see me'; and, 'because I go to the Father'?" So they were saying, "What is this that he says, 'A little while'? We do not know what he is talking about."
Jesus knew that they wished to question him, and he said to them, "Are you deliberating together about this, that I said, 'A little while, and you will not see me, and again a little while, and you will see me'? Truly, truly, I say to you, that you will weep and lament, but the world will rejoice; you will grieve, but your grief will be turned into joy. Whenever a woman is in labour she has pain, because her hour has come; but when she gives birth to the child, she no longer remembers the anguish because of the joy that a child has been born into the world. Therefore you too have grief now; but I will see you again, and your heart will rejoice, and no one will take your joy away from you. In that day you will not question me about anything. Truly, truly, I say to you, if you ask the Father for anything in my name, he will give it to you. Until now you have asked for nothing in my name; ask and you will receive, so that your joy may be made full."[151]*

****

In the midst of a very severe trial, their overflowing joy... welled up[152]

Consider it pure joy, my brothers and sisters, whenever you face trials of many kinds, because you know that the testing

of your faith produces perseverance. Let perseverance fin-
ish its work so that you may be mature and complete, not
lacking anything.[153]

You suffered along with those in prison and joyfully ac-
cepted the confiscation of your property, because you knew
that you yourselves had better and lasting possessions[154]

"Blessed are you when people hate you, when they exclude
you and insult you and reject your name as evil, because of
the Son of Man. Rejoice in that day and leap for joy."[155]

I open with these words, because I want to immediately set the tone for this study, and focus your expectations about this word 'Joy.' If you are reading this chapter in order to receive pointers about how to get happiness, to turn your misfortunes around, or trade your current sufferings for your own immediate relief and satisfaction, you will likely be disappointed. This reflection is not about changing circumstances, but about changing attitudes and perspectives.

It is worthwhile to note from the start that there is a difference between lasting joy and fleeting happiness. It is possible to have moments of happiness without a lasting joy. So too is it possible to be joyful in the absence of immediate happiness.

In this world there is apparently much happiness on offer. 'Buy this product and be happy.' 'Take this this holiday and be happy.' 'Find the perfect partner and be happy.' 'Gain wealth and be happy.' Happiness, as the world sees it, is feeling contentment in the absence of personal dissatisfaction or discomfort.

This is not the joy that we are looking at here. This is not what Jesus is teaching his disciples to seek. Jesus is teaching a lasting and resilient joy. A joy which can shine through our present circumstances, good or bad, because it is built upon eternal truths about our saviour Jesus, and our future inheritance with him. It is a joy formed upon a solid cornerstone. It is an eternal joy, which the immediate cannot subdue.

Yes, you can have joy in pain. Yes, you can have joy in bereavement. Yes, you can have joy through terminal or persistent illness, through poverty, through broken relationships. Yes you can consider it pure joy when you face trials of many kinds. Depending upon what your joy is built.

How many times have you allowed yourself to be robbed of Joy because of unfavourable circumstances? Me? Far too often. Why? Because there is still so much of the world in me - a world that says happiness is found in freedom, in tolerance, in winning your argument, in achieving your ambitions, in being respected, in accumulating possessions. I quickly lose sight of where real joy is found.

But we'll look now at where joy is truly to be found when trials are near, how tears can be turned to joy, and where joy should be anchored even when trials are absent.

Firstly, in times of trial.

Imagine, if you will, that you knew within the next couple of days you would suffer extreme persecution because of your beliefs, and that tonight some officers will come to your door and arrested you for holding those beliefs. You know that the officers will come because one of your own friends had reported you. Imagine you know that, upon witnessing your arrest, all your closest friends will completely abandon you, and that the only voices you will hear on the day of your trial are those of people who despise you. You know that you are innocent, but you know that the judge will be too cowardly to stand up to the crowd. And so you will receive the death penalty. But not before being tortured.

You know in advance that even at the point of your death, your own Father will remove himself from your presence. You know that this will all start tonight. What do you do with your last few hours of freedom?

This, of course, is what will happen to Jesus. Yet, on his last evening as a free man, he chose to sit with his disciples and teach them about how their joy might be complete.

In John 16:16-24, we read Jesus' words to his disciples on this very evening of his betrayal; words that carry on from the last supper, which they have now just left. On this evening, Jesus washed their feet and had communion with them to symbolise his work of salvation. Following this, he goes on to pray for them, and for all who will believe in him through their message. Then he leaves that place to be betrayed by Judas in the garden of Gethsemane.

Let it be recognised that Jesus knew he was going to be betrayed and killed, yet his concern that evening was with matters beyond his immediate circumstances. He was spending time with his friends, using his last night with them before his death to teach them how to be effective and joyful disciples in a fallen, broken world full of people that hated him. He did this because he knew the future impact that these teaching would have.

Throughout this evening there is evidently a frustrated tension as Jesus explains to his disciples the things that will come to pass, yet they cannot grasp them because they cannot see past the 'here and now.' How familiar does this sound to you? Time and time again we see the disciples and Jesus holding a very different perspective from each other. The disciples respond to the immediate consequences of their current events, whilst Jesus is only mindful of those events in relation to their place in the wider context of eternity, and in his future glory.

From this passage we will come to see the importance of our own perspective on current events. This is so crucial in the world in which we live as Christians; as those whose beliefs are contrary -

offensive even - to what is socially acceptable. Rest assured, we will all face trials if we seek to follow Christ wholeheartedly. I pray that I do justice to this passage, because keeping hold of our joy through opposition is ever increasingly a very real challenge to Christians.

Jesus remained faithful to his objective that night in spite of what he knew was coming, because he knew what it would achieve. Throughout his entire ministry, Jesus was never deterred by the opposition and accusations he faced. Not once did he lose sight of his purpose because of anything that was happening in the immediate. Jesus' perspective is an eternal perspective. A biblical perspective. A heavenly perspective. A Godly perspective. This, like his washing of the disciples' feet, was all to set an example to all of his disciples about how we too should live.

Throughout this whole evening, Jesus has carefully laid out for his disciples all that will happen, and its purpose, so that they themselves might be fully equipped for what he is calling them to do. Yet the disciples are only able to focus on the immediate worldly realm. They react in alarm to him washing their feet, to him telling them he is going away in a little while, and to him telling them that they will be hated, persecuted and killed as he is to be. They simply cannot see beyond the moment.

We can sympathise with this. But, a very key element to grasp about joy is that the bigger your perspective, the more room joy has to breathe and be exercised. Yes, if you look at current sufferings for what they are, you will find little room for joy. But if you understand the purpose of these events, or at least trust God that there is indeed a beneficial purpose, joy is to be found in abundance.

When Chris and I were expecting our first child, Chris was terribly ill every waking moment for nine months and two weeks. At the seven- week mark, Chris woke me up and explained to me how she had had a dream in which an angel had appeared to her. The angel said, "You are going to have a girl, and you shall call her Grace, because through her, God will reveal his grace to you."

"Well," we thought. "Lovely!"

After the awful pregnancy, three day labour, and the emergency c-section that was needed to deliver Grace, whom had gone into distress during birth, we were finally delivered our baby girl. We thought, "Now, by God's grace, we will have an easy and joyous time parenting. Perhaps Angels will even sing our daughter to sleep each night, as we recover from this long, difficult ordeal."

Well, we did indeed love parenting our beautiful girl, and still do. But, at nine weeks old, Grace was diagnosed with meningitis. We thought, "God? This is not what we were expecting when you said you'd show us Grace!"

Well, as our daughter was treated and slowly recovered, we came to realise what God was up to. We were visited daily by friends and family from churches all over the place. Some of whom we'd not seen in years. People came out of the woodwork from every-where. We were stunned by the network of support that God had woven around us – a network that we would not have appreciated had we not faced that trial.

To this day we benefit from, and rejoice in, the love and care we are shown by those he has surrounded us with. God has indeed re-vealed to us his love and his grace, and in a way we would never have understood had we not faced the trials.

Remember what James says on the matter. Trials should be re-ceived with joy, in the understanding that through them you are being richly blessed with the opportunity to develop persever-ance and, through that, be made mature and complete, not lack-ing anything.

Having a wrong understanding of the joy Jesus taught not only leads us to miss the joy to be known in hardships, but it also causes us to misdirect our joy in our successes. Remember the passage in Luke, where Jesus sent out the seventy-two, and they returned with joy because they had been able to cast out demons. Jesus tells them,

> *"do not rejoice that the spirits submit to you, but rejoice that your names are written in heaven."[156]*

The clear message here is, 'broaden your perspective.' Do not let your joy be dependant upon what is happening today, but let it rest upon matters of eternity.

Looking more closely at John chapter 16:16, Jesus says,

> *"In a little while you will see me no more, and then after a little while you will see me."*

The common view is that this refers to the time when Jesus is taken to be crucified, and the time when he will appear to them after his resurrection. The disciples however do not understand this and so keep asking each-other what he could mean. Jesus saw that they wanted to ask him about this, but are reluctant.

I mentioned the dynamic of tension, confusion and grief amongst the disciples and, in part, this is perhaps due to the fact that, in his own words, Jesus has been speaking figuratively (v25). The disciples had simply been unable to unravel the meaning of Jesus' words. Jesus knows what they are thinking, however, and saves them asking him. He responds by taking the question accurately from their lips, and graciously giving the answer in such a way as to shed light upon his motives throughout.

Such was his ability to determine what they were asking amongst themselves, and such the manner of his reply, that the disciples say,

"Now you are speaking clearly and without figures of speech. Now we can see that you know all things and that you do not even need anyone to ask you questions."[157]

Before a word is on my tongue, you Lord know it completely. [158]

In this moment, the disciples have a deeper understanding of what Jesus has been teaching about himself,. They say,

"This makes us believe that you came from God."[159]

Jesus is able to tell the disciples that which they are being careful to avoid him hearing. In light of this we note that it is foolishness to try and hide from Jesus what you are thinking, doing, or saying. He knows your words before they are on your tongue.

You may have any number of questions for God,

"Why all the suffering, Lord?"
"Why was that person never healed?"
"Where were you during my trial?"

You may even have questions about whether or not he exists. He knows your questions, and is eager to meet you where you are; to answer your questions; to draw you closer to himself; to reveal who he is. Don't hide your questions from him, lest he hide from you the answers!

Having correctly revealed their question, Jesus starts his reply with this..

"Very truly I tell you, you will weep and mourn while the world rejoices. You will grieve but your grief will turn to Joy."[160]

Jesus knew that he was going to the cross, and that he would rise from death. He tells the disciples quite plainly in Matthew 17:22,

> *"The son of man is going to be delivered into the hands of men. They will kill him, and on the third day he will be raised to life."*

The verse goes on to say,

> *The disciples were filled with grief.*

Jesus says he will die and rise again. It seems the disciples hear only that he will die, and are filled with grief. How easy we find it to focus on our tragedy and grieve, when there is wonder to be found in the resurrection and all it means for us. The host of heaven proclaim without ceasing the glorious resurrection and kingship of Jesus - a kingship that pronounces freedom over us; an entitlement as heirs in his kingdom; gifts of the Spirit; life everlasting. But, how easy it is to focus primarily on what we stand to lose, suffer, and struggle with.

Jesus said,

> *"let the dead bury their dead, but you go and proclaim the kingdom of God."[161]*

Let the worldly focus on the world, but let those who are chosen look first at the kingdom.

> *Rejoice in the Lord always. I will say it again: Rejoice! Let your gentleness be evident to all. The Lord is near. Do not be anxious about anything, but in every situation, by prayer and petition, with thanksgiving, present your requests to*

God. And the peace of God, which transcends all under-
standing, will guard your hearts and your minds in Christ
Jesus.

Finally, brothers and sisters, whatever is true, whatever
is noble, whatever is right, whatever is pure, whatever is
lovely, whatever is admirable—if anything is excellent or
praiseworthy—think about such things.[162]

Jesus told his disciples,

"You will weep and mourn while the world rejoices.... Now
is your time of grief, but I will see you again and you will re-
joice, and no one will take away your joy."[163]

'You will see me die and will grieve,' says Jesus, 'whilst the world who didn't want to know me will rejoice.' Jesus is giving a clear message regarding the disciples' mourning and joy. When Jesus seems removed from us we will mourn, and when we see him we shall be filled with a joy that no one will take away.

Does this not ring true with you? When trials of this life take our focus off of God - when, in our hardships, we cannot see Jesus - we mourn and weep and grieve. But when we are truly in close communion with him, seeing Jesus within our trials, how much our burden is lifted and he turns our tears to joy.

To explain how their tears will indeed turn to joy, Jesus gives the disciples the example of a woman giving birth. He says that she has pain because her time has come, but when her baby is delivered she forgets the anguish because of her joy that her child is born into the world. It is through her pain that her baby is born. And when it arrives, she forgets her pain, because of her joy.

How many times have you thought that you would be completely overwhelmed by circumstances, and then, when you are enjoying the fruits of you labour, you forget quite how bad the pain ever was? Note that by using the words, "she has pain because her time has come," Jesus again points to himself. He has used the same expression about himself in relation to the cross. Through the pains of his labour, he will give birth to his people. Life to his family. And his pain will then be forgotten.

Remember this example of the mother giving birth, and the joy she has in her child, when you are ever tempted to despair or even into anger towards God for letting you go through trials. If you are angry or overwhelmed, it is a sign that perhaps your focus needs to be put back onto Jesus, and your efforts better spent remembering what he has achieved for you.

If you are suffering now, look forward. If you are holding on to the memory of past suffering, then you are not fully enjoying the fruit of your labour - the purpose for the pain - and you need to stop looking back! Trials are hard, but If we take our eyes off of Jesus, we risk starting to wander from him. That is what happened at the point of Jesus' death. The disciples scattered. Jesus had said that they would, in verse 32,

> *"A time is coming and in fact has come when you will be scattered, each of you to your own home. You will leave me all alone."*

And they did. They took their eyes off Jesus, and lost sight of what he had said was being achieved through his death. His actions were affecting their greatest freedom and fullest life, but they can only feel trapped, and see bleakest death. Their life is just beginning, but they feel it is falling apart.

Are you so caught up on what is happening in your life today, that you can't see God's purposes? Are you tempted to despair over that which is happening now, or does your faith in God's agenda lift you above it, into rejoicing?

> *In all things God works for the good of those who love him, who have been called according to his purpose.[164]*

Do you believe it?

Jesus is the good shepherd. He will not allow his flock to remain scattered. He went out into the world to rescue his sheep, guiding them back toward their safe pastures. Shall we then despair over what seems to be going wrong now, or shall we rejoice that, if we stay true to God, he will guide his flock in peace and safety and joy?

TEARS TO JOY, PART TWO

John 16:23-24

"In that day, you will no longer ask me anything. Very truly I tell you, my Father will give you whatever you ask in my name. Until now you have not asked anything in my name."[165]

*****

Until this point in Jesus' ministry, anything that the disciples have done of any power, has been by Jesus' command and anointing. But when the disciples received for themselves the Spirit of God, they were then able to ask the Father for anything in Jesus name, and it was done. So it is with us. If we ask anything in the name of Jesus, the Father will give it.

Now this is not licence to ask for all manner of things at the prompting of our own selfish desires, using Jesus' name as a magic word to unlock our every desire. What Jesus is saying is that if we ask in his name, i.e. in for his purposes, according to his will, and for his glory, then it will be given. So writes James,

You do not have because you do not ask God. When you ask, you do not receive, because you ask with wrong motives, that you may spend what you get on your pleasures.[166]

But,

"If you remain in me and my words remain in you, ask whatever you wish, and it will be done for you."[167]

"and then your joy will be complete."[168]

Do you want your joy to be complete? Understand this - Jesus died and was resurrected, and ascended back to the Father from whom he came. He sent to us the Holy Spirit to guide us into all truth. What the Spirit of truth speaks is only that which he has received from Jesus. All that belongs to the Father belongs to Jesus, and belongs to the Spirit which lives within you. Remain in Jesus, not in the world. Have his words remain in you, and overrule your own. Use those words to ask of him, and you will receive with fullness of joy.

No-one has ever sought the Father's will more selflessly than Jesus which is why throughout his ministry all that he asked was done for him. On this very night, Jesus asked the Father to take his cup from him; to remove from him the trial that he faced. And yet, he then says,

> *"not my will but yours be done."[169]*

The cup was not taken from him because it was not the Father's will. It was the Father's will for Jesus to overcome the world. It was the Father's will for Jesus to die, so that the power of the enemy will no longer have a hold on us. We have all sinned and fallen short of the glory of God. The only way that we would have any right to a relationship and eternity with our God in heaven, is if Jesus gave himself to die, that God might accept his body and blood as a sacrifice on our behalf if we fully give our lives to him and trust in his death and resurrection for our own salvation. That was the Father's will, and that is what Jesus subjected him-self to, so that we might be saved. Jesus submitted himself to the Father's will even unto death. That is a great challenge to our own level of commitment, selflessness, and subjection to the Father's will.

If you do not know this salvation, where is your joy? That lasting joy that reigns through any and every circumstance and trial that this world throws at you? This joy cannot yet be yours, since it can only be built upon Jesus. It is a chief weapon of your enemy to have you so caught up in the events of this world, that you are too distracted to realise there is a saviour, and that you need him.

Trust in the fickle joy that Satan offers you through this world, and you will spend your eternity with him. Trust in the lasting joy of the resurrection of Jesus, and you will spend your eternity with him. It is your choice, and if there is any conviction in your heart now about choosing Jesus as your saviour, you must act upon it. Invite God to come and take the place of the enemy as the possessor of your life.

Every page in the Bible points to the day that Jesus would come and deliver God's people from their ultimate enemy Satan, so that all the power of death and hell would be thrown down under Jesus' feet, for his glory and for the deliverance of God's people. It is what every one of our momentary trials point to - that day in which we are delivered from our ultimate problem of sin and death. This is where our joy is found, not merely in God bringing us through our momentary trials, but that our very lives have been pulled out of the fires of hell, and we've been given a dwelling place in the presence of the almighty.

The prophet Jeremiah speaks of all this, and his words ring true all throughout history. They describe what God has done in the past for his people Israel, they describe what God did when Jesus lived and died and raised to life again, and they describe what will happen on the coming day of judgement. What Jeremiah speaks of Jacob and Israel – God's people – and their relief from physical, momentary foes, is now true of all his people, and speaks of their eternal destiny, and relief from spiritual warfare.

> *He who scattered Israel, will gather them, and watch over his flock like a shepherd. For the Lord will deliver Jacob and redeem them from those stronger than they. They will come and shout for Joy on the heights of Zion; They will rejoice in the bounty of the Lord- The grain, the new wine, and the*

olive oil. The young of the flocks and herds. They will be like a well watered garden, and they will sorrow no more. Then young women will dance and be glad, young men and old as well.

I will turn their mourning into gladness; I will give them comfort and joy instead of sorrow. I will satisfy the priests with abundance, and my people will be filled with my bounty,"

Declares the lord.[170]

God's message, which is consistent throughout history, is that he shall rescue those who put their trust in him, and reward their trust abundantly. Does he promise that you wont have trials? No. Does he promise that you will not mourn? No. If fact, he promised that in this world you *will* have trouble. He says, 'the world hated me, and so it will hate you. The world persecuted me, so it will persecute you'. He says a time is coming when people who kill you will think that they are doing a service for God. Look around you today. Christians are being persecuted, tortured and killed by religious extremists who think that they are *serving* God!

In this world you will have trouble...

Blessed are you when you face trials of many kinds. God uses trials to develop your perseverance and maturity, so that you will lack nothing. Jesus promised that your tears will be turned to joy, if not in this life, then for eternity afterwards. Jesus overcame this world so that you could too.

...but take heart, I have overcome this world.[171]

Jesus' message is consistent throughout his ministry. We've been considering John 13-16, Jesus' last sermon. Let's look at his first:

> *Blessed are the poor in Spirit*
> *for theirs is the kingdom of heaven.*
> *Blessed are those who mourn,*
> *for they will be comforted.*
> *Blessed are the meek,*
> *for they will inherit the earth.*
> *Blessed are those who hunger and thirst for*
> *righteousness.*
> *Blessed are the pure in heart, are the peacemakers, are those*
> *who are persecuted because of*
> *righteousness.*
> *Blessed are you when people insult you, persecute you and*
> *falsely say all kinds of evil against you because of me.[172]*

Jesus says all the way through, 'Blessed *are* you... for you *will* receive'. Consider yourself blessed *now*, because of what *will* come. Your blessing is a future reward for what you are now going through.

> *'Rejoice and be glad,' he says, 'because great is your reward*
> *in heaven.'[173]*

Fix your eyes and your hope on your saviour, and on the kingdom of heaven. Your tears will be turned to joy, and it is a joy no one can take away. And do you know what Jesus says immediately afterwards, about people who are well off now?

> *"Woe to you who are rich,*
> *for you have already received your comfort.*
> *Woe to you who are well fed now,*
> *for you will go hungry.*

> *Woe to you who laugh now,*
> *for you will mourn and weep.*
> *Woe to you when everyone speaks well of you,*
> *for that is how their ancestors treated the false*
> *prophets."[174]*

So, what of those who are content with living in happiness now? I don't know about you, but I like to not be hungry, I like to laugh, I like the thought of everyone speaking well of me. These things all make me happy, and in themselves are not a bad thing. But, if I am always well fed and always laughing, always in prosperity and well received, it is likely because I am keeping for myself everything God has entrusted to me, and perhaps never challenging the destructive worldliness around me with the gospel?

There are people who could be well fed, but go hungry because they have committed themselves to ensuring that others have food. There are those who do not laugh with the world, but stand against it. There are those who could be very popular and have others speak well of them, but they commit themselves to truly presenting the gospel, and so face ridicule and persecution.

In 1 Corinthians 7, Paul says that people who are happy ought to live as if they were not! At first glance this is hard to understand. Should those who are happy, mope around and pretend to be sad? This is as futile as people who misunderstand Jesus' teaching about joy. Wearing a fake frown is as worthless as wearing a fake smile. Paul's argument is that time is short, and the world in its present from is passing away. We should, therefore, not be so engrossed with our current circumstances, living in the happiness which this world affords us, but be ever mindful of eternal matters.

Have you happiness in worldly pleasures? You are at risk of receiving your comfort here, at the expense of your comfort in heaven?

Are you happy with your bank balance? Then give, and give, and give. Give to those who are poor all around you. Give until your bank balance truly requires you to ask God for provision.

Are you happy with your possessions? Then give more to those who have a real need for them. Give your things away, until you can earnestly pray, 'Jehovah Jireh, I am needy, please give me today my daily bread.'

Are you happy with the friendship group you have built around you? Extend it to include those with whom you don't click so easily, and those who you see sitting alone. Befriend those whom others reject.

Are you happy because you can regularly fill your stomach? Fast more. Rule over your body so that you know what it is to hunger and thirst. Then use that hunger for food to motivate your prayers for righteousness.

Are you happy with how you behave? Pray that in his mercy, God would reveal your sin. If you say you have no sin, you deceive yourself and the truth is not in you. Allow him to convict you. If we confess, he is faithful to forgive.

Are you happy with your world? Ask God to open your eyes to the devastation all around; the millions of people throughout the world who are headed for eternal damnation. And be prepared to pray, 'God, send me to them, having equipped me to do as you have commanded, to take your gospel to the ends of the world.

The parable of the talents suggests that those who invest what they have been given are good and faithful and will be given more, but those who are happy to keep hold of what they are given, are wicked and lazy and will have it taken from them.

Jesus invested his life for us; Greater love has no one than this. Invest wholeheartedly in others, good and faithful servant, loving others as Christ has loved you. By this they will know you are his disciples, and you will be given more from heaven's bounty.

This is not a prosperity gospel. If you are only giving to gain more worldly possessions, you are not truly loving others and you disqualify yourself. Instead, build up treasures in heaven, by loving people. What you do for the least of these, you do for me, says Jesus. You are blessed, they are blessed, and God is blessed. It is joy for you, joy for them, and joy for Christ.

If your joy is bound up in things of this earth, which moths destroy and robbers steal, then it will be taken from you. But Joy that is bound to a closeness with Jesus, is a joy that no one will ever take away. Are you troubled in this world? Rejoice for your place in the next. Are you sure of that joy you have without Jesus as your saviour? Your treasure is fit only for the moths and robbers.

I implore you... Ask God to remove worldly happiness from you. Ask him to make you less comfortable. Ask him to allow trials that lead you to completeness, under his protection. Ask him to know what it is to face trouble because of your righteousness. In this world real Christians will have trouble, but take heart, says Jesus, I have overcome the world. Keep your eyes firmly fixed upon the kingdom of God, and you will overcome the world too. Your tears will truly be turned to joy.

The seed which falls on rocky ground, springs up but lasts only a short time because it has no root. Do we want to be those who hear God's word and receive it with joy, but quickly fall away when trouble or persecution comes because of the world?

It is only by God's guidance and empowerment that we can do his will, to glorify him and know real lasting joy. Ask for this now. Ask the Father to align your heart with his own and help you remain in him, his word alive in you, that you may follow his commands, loving him and one another, for his great glory.

[1] Galatians 5:22-25

[2] Genesis 1:28

[3] Numbers 13:27

[4] Leviticus 25, 26

[5] Deuteronomy 28

[6] Isaiah 11:1

[7] Isaiah 27:6

[8] Isaiah 37:31

[9] Mark 8:22-26

[10] Matthew 3:7

[11] Philippians 2:12

[12] Matthew 23:33

[13] Matthew 7:15-23

[14] Matthew 21:43

[15] 2 Corinthians 5:20

[16] 1 Corinthians 4:16-17

[17] Matthew 7:18

[18] John 16:33

[19] Isaiah 26:3

[20] Romans 12:2

[21] James 1:2 [paraphrased]

[22] Romans 8:37

[23] 1 Corinthians 4:12

[24] 2 Corinthians 6:4-7

[25] John 15:5

[26] Matthew 5:23-24

[27]   Genesis 1:1

[28]   Genesis 1:3-4

[29]   Genesis 1:6-7

[30]   Genesis 1:14,17-18

[31]   Genesis 13

[32]   Genesis 25:23

[33]   Genesis 30

[34]   Genesis 4:10

[35]   Genesis 4:25

[36]   Genesis 5:18-20

[37]   Genesis 5:21

[38]   Genesis 5:22

[39]   Genesis 5:23-24

[40]   Psalm 84:10

[41]   James 5:17

[42]   Matthew 5:48

[43]   2 Peter 3:10

[44]   Colossians 3:5-10

[45]   Jude 14-16

[46]   Jude 11

[47]   1 John 1:5-6

[48]   1 John 1:7

[49]   Proverbs 15:10

[50]   Romans 3:23

[51]   Psalm 23:3

[52]   Joshua 22:5

[53]   Genesis 16:1-2

[54]   Genesis 15:1

[55]   Genesis 15:2-3

[56]   Genesis 15:5

[57]   Genesis 16:1-2

[58]   Genesis 26:2

[59]   Genesis 16:10

[60]   Genesis 12:1-3

[61]   Genesis 12:7

[62]   Deuteronomy 31:6

[63] 1 John 2:17
[64] Jeremiah 29:11
[65] Malachi 3:1
[66] Leviticus 26:12
[67] Malachi 2:4,5
[68] Malachi 3:6
[69] Malachi 2:16
[70] Malachi 3:2
[71] Malachi 3:2,3
[72] Romans 12:1
[73] Malachi 3:3
[74] Philippians 4:13
[75] 2 Corinthians 5:17
[76] Romans 12:1-2
[77] Malachi 3:10
[78] Malachi 2:17
[79] Malachi 2:17
[80] Daniel 7:25-27
[81] Daniel 7:18
[82] John 3:16:17
[83] Proverbs 12:1
[84] Hebrews 11:6
[85] Matthew 2:1-12
[86] Luke 2:8-18
[87] Matthew 23:12
[88] John 12:25
[89] John14:16
[90] Matthew 5:3
[91] John 3:16
[92] Luke 2:8-18
[93] Romans 12:2
[94] Luke 2:41-47
[95] Luke 2:48
[96] Luke 2:49
[97] Luke 19:28-38
[98] Luke 19:11

[99]   Luke 18:32

[100]   Joshua 10:16-27

[101]   John 2:19

[102]   Revelation 7:9-10

[103]   John 12:13

[104]   2 Samuel 6:21-22

[105]   Luke 19:41

[106]   Luke 17:11

[107]   Luke 19:11-27

[108]   Romans 12:2

[109]   2 Corinthians 5

[110]   John 11:1-4

[111]   John 11:4

[112]   John 11:23

[113]   John 11:24

[114]   John 11:25-26

[115]   John 11:26

[116]   John 11:26

[117]   John 11:14-15

[118]   John 11:35

[119]   John 11:38

[120]   John 11:39

[121]   John 11:39

[122]   John 11:40

[123]   John 11:40

[124]   John 11:41

[125]   John 11:41-42

[126]   John 11:42

[127]   John 11:43

[128]   John 11:44

[129]   John 11:44

[130]   John 13:1-5

[131]   Isaiah 63:15

[132]   Exodus 7:1-4

[133]   Isaiah 43:18-28

[134]   John 10:31-33

[135] Matthew 16:15-22

[136] John 12:13

[137] John 13:1

[138] John 13:5

[139] John 13:3

[140] John 13:17

[141] Philippians 2:3-5

[142] John 1:2-4, Hebrews 1:3, Hebrews 2:14, Luke 2:12, Philippians 2:6-11, Romans 3:25, 1 Peter 3:18, John 19:30, Philippians 2:6-11, Revelation 1:13-16, Philippians 2:6-11.

[143] Matthew 20:28, Galatians 5:13, 1 Peter 4:10, 1 Peter 5:2-3, 1 Timothy 3:13, Romans 12:10-11

[144] Isaiah 61:10

[145] Luke 24:49

[146] John 20:23

[147] John 13:16

[148] John 13:8

[149] John 13:9

[150] John 13:10

[151] John 16:16-24

[152] 2 Corinthians 8:2

[153] James 1:2-4

[154] Hebrews 10:34

[155] Luke 6:22

[156] Luke 10:20

[157] John 16:29-30

[158] Psalm 139

[159] John 16:30

[160] John 16:20

[161] Matthew 8:22

[162] Philippians 4:4-8

[163] John 16:20,22

[164] Romans 8:28

[165] John 16:23-24

[166] James 4:2-3

[167] John 15:11

Paul Muzzall

[168] John 16:24
[169] Luke 22:42
[170] Jeremiah 31:10-14
[171] John 16:33
[172] Matthew 5:3-11
[173] Matthew 5:12
[174] Luke 6:24-26

Printed in Poland
by Amazon Fulfillment
Poland Sp. z o.o., Wrocław